GOTTSCHALK
SERVANT OF GOD

GOTTSCHALK
SERVANT OF GOD

A Story of Courage, Faith, and Love for the Truth

written and illustrated by
CONNIE L. MEYER

REFORMED
FREE PUBLISHING
ASSOCIATION
Jenison, Michigan

Cover design by Erika Kiel
Cover illustration by Connie L. Meyer
Interior design by Katherine Lloyd, The DESK

Reformed Free Publishing Association
1894 Georgetown Center Drive
Jenison, Michigan 49428
616-457-5970
www.rfpa.org

ISBN: 978-1-936054-88-6
Ebook ISBN: 978-1-936054-89-3
LCCN: 2015948900

to my children,
grandchildren,
and children in the Lord

CONTENTS

PREFACE

hy a story about Gottschalk? Mysteries still surround the life of the medieval monk named Gottschalk. Letters concerning his teaching have been found just in the past century. Drawings included in the book to illustrate the story are only an artist's conception. Perhaps more facts pertaining to this preacher of predestination will yet come to light. Nevertheless, the story of this man, this important man—this often forgotten and misunderstood man—must be told. The links in the chain of church history are not complete without him.

From the time the truth of the gospel was made clear to the New Testament saints in Jerusalem and beyond, and the Nicene Council fought for the truth of the divinity of Jesus Christ in 325, and Augustine battled to maintain the truths of sovereign grace in the fifth century against Pelagius, little development happened in defense of the truth until the time of Luther and Calvin in the sixteenth century. Little, that is, except for Gottschalk. Even Luther and Calvin were not aware of Gottschalk and his stand for the truth of sovereign grace and predestination. Had they known of him, they would have rejoiced.

One might wonder, had God forgotten his church in all those centuries between? Was the truth anywhere to be found or to be preached? The Roman Catholic Church had already begun to decline. The seeds of man's ability to save himself, the seeds sown by Augustine's archenemy, Pelagius, steadily sprang up as poisonous weeds even while Augustine lived. And weeds grow.

But the truth was still in the hearts and minds of God's people. God was putting it there. Gottschalk is evidence of that.

God was protecting his church, preserving her, leading her, guiding her. No, she was not forgotten. God was leading her throughout all of history, sometimes at a crawl, sometimes at a trot, and sometimes at a grueling gallop—but he was with her all along. Such is the comfort we receive from the story of Gottschalk. God preserves his church. As Gottschalk would say in his characteristic way, "It is obviously seen brighter than the sun and is more clearly apparent than daylight."[1]

ACKNOWLEDGMENTS

Because of the unique character of Gottschalk's story, a note about the bibliography and references in this book is in order. This story could not have been told without the important work of previous authors and historians. This is especially true because not a great amount of material is available about Gottschalk, particularly in English. This makes what sources are available to be very important indeed.

Ronald Hanko has translated some of Gottschalk's writings from Latin, and with his gracious permission, his translation of Gottschalk's *Shorter Confession* is included at the end of this book, while his translations of Gottschalk's *Longer* and *Shorter Confessions* and *Extant Fragments* are available electronically as bonus material at www.rfpa.org. Victor Genke and Francis X. Gumerlock have also written about and translated some of Gottschalk's writings. Their book, entitled *Gottschalk and a Medieval Predestination Controversy*, was an important source for this story. So were the chapter on Gotteschalk in Herman Hanko's *Portraits of Faithful Saints* and the chapter on Rabanus Maurus in Hanko's *Contending for the Faith*. The bibliography at the end of this book gives a complete list of sources used, although more could be especially acknowledged here.

Kirsten De Vries very ably gave of her time and expertise in various languages to assist in translating some of the sources that could only be found in German, as well as helped to determine how to reference pronunciations of foreign words included in the story.

The English language, however, does not contain all sounds as they are authentically spoken in foreign lands, so some pronunciations are only approximate.

Along with the translated material already mentioned, two poems written by Gottschalk are included at the end of this book. Working from classical Latin to translate medieval poetry is no easy task. I am greatly indebted to Jason Holstege, Jonathan Langerak, Jr., and Justin Smidstra for their time, effort, and expertise given in this important endeavor.

Marvin Kamps, now in glory, read the manuscript and provided very helpful suggestions and encouragement. Several junior high readers also read the manuscript and jotted down questions or comments along the way. The work of these readers, younger and older, proved to be invaluable and surely has contributed to a much improved book.

Nor can I underestimate the great encouragement and sound, godly advice of a beloved friend, Dena Engelsma, who is also now in glory. Her knowledge and love of literature and poetry were irreplaceable. Her comments always instructive; her wit always delightful—she was helpful even to the very last days of her life. She is appreciated more than words can say.

One's family as well is never left untouched in such a project. I am much indebted to my husband and children. They too were not left out of the evaluation process, and their opinions and suggestions were also very helpful, as well as their modeling for illustrations. I could mention many others besides, such as friends and family, who gave an encouraging word, and librarians who helped find sources.

A work such as this is not brought to publication alone. With many thanks and much credit to all these and more, the following story is submitted to the reader.

INTRODUCTION

Those were the days of knights, of kings and queens, and of dynasties. Those were the days of lords and serfs, of monks and nuns, and of Vikings, when monasteries were many and the church and governors of the land shared rule.

Some people call those days the Dark Ages. The days were dark in a way, dark to us. It was so long ago, the details of the history are hard to know. The days were spiritually dark as well. True doctrine was hard to come by, if not nearly lost.

But there was a light. A clear beam of understanding and truth reflected from one monastery, from one courtroom, from one dungeon—from one man. This is a story of courage, of faith, and of love for the truth. This is the story of Gottschalk, the monk from Orbais (Or-BAY).

A knight from the ninth century, ready for battle.

And I will walk at liberty
Because Thy truth I seek;
Thy truth before the kings of earth
With boldness I will speak.

—Psalter 326:3 (versification of Psalm 119:45–46)

CHAPTER 1

Charlemagne (Shar-la-MANE) was a mighty king and ruler who stood almost seven feet tall. He looked as mighty as he was. He spent most of his reign, which was from 768 to 814, going forth to conquer neighboring lands. He won almost every battle. By the time of his death he ruled all of western Europe.

Charlemagne did other important things as well. He belonged to the Christian church of that day, so he was concerned about Christian things. He did not want the people he conquered to be completely destroyed or to be slaves. He wanted all those people to be Christians, and he wanted to rule over them that way. When each heathen, idol-worshiping tribe was conquered, he forced the people to convert to Christianity and to be baptized. If they refused, they could be killed. Later Charlemagne sent missionaries to each of those lands to teach the people there what it meant to be a Christian.

How genuine these kinds of conversions were is highly questionable from our viewpoint in history. However, many of the people he conquered did in time come to believe as Christians, at least in part. Charlemagne allowed them to "Christianize" many of their pagan practices, so their change to Christianity was not always a complete change of heart. Yet their change of religion did help to make Charlemagne's rule more peaceful and secure. His subjects could better understand his laws.

But this tall and mighty ruler was not content to conquer only heathens and lands. He wanted to conquer more. He wanted to conquer ignorance. Although he could read Latin, he could not even write his name. Many in those days could not read or write. That was of great concern to Charlemagne. He wanted the people in his realm to be educated.

He gathered the most famous and best teachers in all the land to come to his palace in Aachen (Ah-ken) to start a royal school there. Men who were taught in this school would be educated enough to be able to help govern the land and to be bishops and abbots in the church. In 789 Charlemagne decreed that every monastery in his domain must maintain schools for the children, whether they lived in the monastery or not. Education must be for all.

Toward the end of Charlemagne's reign a remarkable thing happened. Charlemagne came to Rome to visit the pope of the church and to worship with him. It was Christmas day in the year 800, and Pope Leo III had something special planned for that day. During the Christmas service the pope crowned Charlemagne to be the Holy Roman emperor. Charlemagne may not have been aware that this was going to happen, but it happened all the same.

The pope took the authority not only to say who would be king, but also to say who would be the godlike emperor over the whole realm. And the king, then called an emperor, took the authority to accept the honor of that title and to protect the pope. Each man depended on the other, but at the same time each man wanted to rule over the other. Such rivalries would continue in Europe for centuries.

Those were the early Middle Ages, when there was little separation between the state government and the church, when fierce Vikings

Charlemagne's throne at Aachen.

from the north raided and attacked any town at any time, when plagues came and went and left hundreds of graves in their wake, when monasteries dotted the land like leopard spots, and when only one church existed in all of western Europe—the Roman Catholic Church. Those were interesting times in which to live. Those were difficult times in which to live. Those were dangerous times in which to live.

Into those times in 806 an infant boy named Gottschalk (GOTT-chalk) was born.[1]

5

CHAPTER 2

Count Bernus and his wife received their newborn son from the Lord. They named him Gottschalk, meaning servant of God. Although they were Saxons who descended from a line of pagan, idol-worshiping tribes in what is today Germany, they lived in Charlemagne's Frankish territory then. Charlemagne had conquered that area and brought the Christian religion into it. Count Bernus, probably of noble Saxon heritage, was appointed to the stately, regal position of count after Charlemagne took over. Bernus was loyal to Charlemagne and to the new faith that this new king brought to his conquered land. By their choosing the name Gottschalk, we know that God was in the mind of those parents as they welcomed their precious baby boy into the world.

Count Bernus and his wife received their son from the Lord.

A count in those days was a high-ranking official who ruled an area of land on behalf of the king. Counts had charge over a county, an area surrounding a city or fortress, or a number of towns or villages. Bernus owned a large manor or castle, land, horses, and servants. If he lived in a castle, it most likely was constructed of wood rather than stone, because most of the buildings at that time were wooden. Many castles would be built in the next century, and most of them would be built of stone. However the count's dwelling was built, it was a fine home. He was a nobleman who was rich in this world's goods as well as rich in political power.

A count usually had much for his children to inherit. Gottschalk's father did too. Gottschalk could have been brought up in all the luxuries that the early Middle Ages had to offer: soft fur blankets, fine linen clothes, carved wooden furniture, roasted meats, pastries, and more. Many people were very poor in the Middle Ages, but some were very rich. Gottschalk was born into one of the richest of homes.

Charlemagne is known as the first ruling Frank, establishing the Frankish dynasty, the ruling family tree of the Franks. This is a coin from that time, depicting this mighty ruler.

All this could mean that Gottschalk might be wealthy all his life and that he might receive some sort of official position and lands when he grew up. He could raise a family of his own to carry on the family name; he could own property and have political power. Or he could become a knight to serve and protect his king.

But he also might not do any of those things or have any of those things. Many children of noble birth did not. Many would live in anything but luxury and comfort, with barely a blanket to stay warm in winter and no earthly possessions to their name but the cloaks on their backs. Gottschalk would be one of those.

How could this be? We know a large inheritance belonged to Gottschalk—large enough to be part of a serious dispute later on. So what would account for his birth into a rich and powerful family but living in extreme poverty and discomfort, even as a child?

Gottschalk's parents believed they were doing great service to God by donating their son along with his inheritance to the church.

That was their plan with Gottschalk. Perhaps that was the reason they named him servant of God. They knew where he would go.

Many noblemen did that. Monasteries and convents were not filled with many beggars, poor, and outcast; they were filled with men and women of noble and mighty birth. Joining a monastery usually involved paying a fee, a sum of money the poor could not afford. Besides, joining a monastery was seen as a holy thing to do. The rich had more to lose to prove such holiness. One who went to live in a monastery must give up all earthly possessions and focus on God alone, joining to pray and worship at least seven times each day. A life of self-sacrifice it certainly was, and many wanted to live that way.

Perhaps they made vows to live in such a manner out of sincere love and devotion to God. Perhaps they made such vows to try to earn their salvation from God. Perhaps an older brother was going to receive all the family's inheritance and the best option left was to join a monastery and try to gain a high position in the church. Whatever their thoughts were about the matter, many chose to live and pray and work in these quiet, solemn buildings and chapels set apart from the world for such purposes.

"Indoors I suffer the icy cold, the sight of my frozen bed gives no pleasure, warm neither when I get up nor where I sleep, I snatch what rest I can." [1]

But some did not choose this life for themselves. Some were brought as young children to live within the quiet, cold walls. Gottschalk would be one of those.

Gottschalk. Servant of God. His parents could not have known how fitting his name would be. The abbot of his monastery would never understand. But God knew his name. God knew his name from all eternity. God would make his name true.

CHAPTER 3

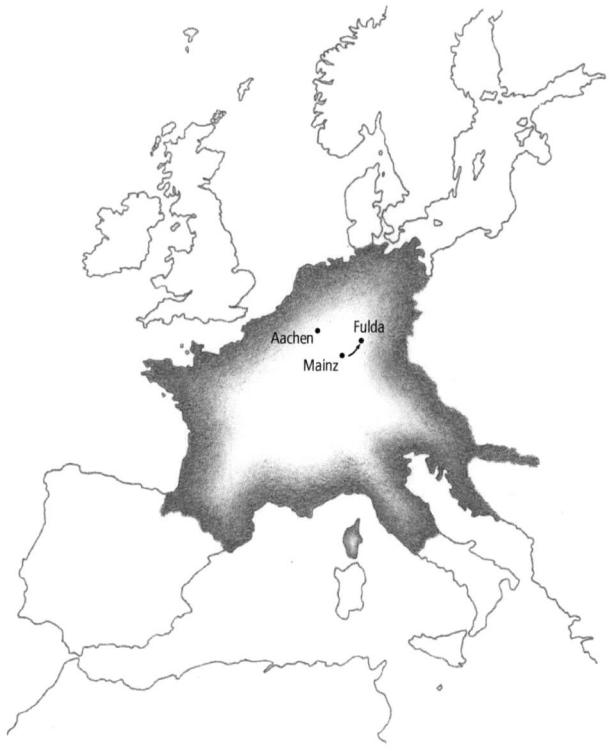

Charlemagne, the tall and mighty ruler of the Holy Roman Empire, was going to die. God had given him a long life and reign. A grand funeral procession would mark the burial of this important man in history, while the rule of the empire would pass peacefully to his son, Louis the Pious. The year was 814. Times in western Europe were going to change.

Changes were going to gradually be seen in the whole empire, but changes—drastic changes—were already happening about that time for one boy who lived in the Saxon part of Charlemagne's kingdom. Gottschalk could have been as young as seven years old when his parents prepared to travel with him from their home in Mainz (Mine-ts) to the monastery in Fulda. Gottschalk must come along, but Gottschalk would not return home with them again.

Gottschalk must come along, but Gottschalk would not return home again.

Children of noblemen were often sent away to be educated, sometimes to another nobleman's home to be tutored there, or more often to a monastery school—to not only learn there, but also to be a member there. That is how the children of the rich were educated in the Middle Ages. But we can only guess at the thoughts of parents who brought their children away at such a time and the emotions of the children so young who must leave their families.

How does one explain to a little boy that he will never again live at home in his large and beautiful house and never again be in close company with his parents and brothers and sisters? He must go to live with strangers, in service to God, and his life must be strictly ordered as the church says it must be. All his inheritance will be given to the monastery where he will live out his days, never to marry, never to own one object of beauty or worth, much less own one inch of land or property. The church will own him and all his possessions. He will be raised to obey the church in all things. Prayer will be central to every day, and utter silence will be required at every meal, with studying, working, and copying manuscripts in between. This is how monks lived. Gottschalk must learn to be a monk.

Young boys who were brought to live in monasteries were

The monastery and cathedral complex that exists in Fulda today was rebuilt and remodeled in 1712. Two huge towers dominate the architecture of the present cathedral, and those towers replaced two that existed on the same spot and belonged to the original eighth-century building.

called oblates. The practice was not unusual. Other oblates were already living in the Fulda monastery. In fact, Fulda was known for its education. Gottschalk's father might have felt proud to bring his son to such a famous and prestigious place of religious instruction. Fulda was one of the best. Later Gottschalk would appreciate that part of his life, but at this time, all he knew were changes.

A monastery still stands in Fulda, the place where Gottschalk was ceremonially handed over to the church by his parents.

In 744, about seventy years before Gottschalk arrived, St. Boniface, the famous missionary to the German Saxons, had founded the abbey. Boniface wanted Fulda, which was located on the border of wild Saxon country, to be an especially important abbey in the whole of Charlemagne's empire. Boniface made sure the

Abbey is another word for a monastery, where monks (men and boys) live under the direction of an abbot (a word meaning father). The monks take vows to maintain a secluded and holy life.

11

monastery was built with extra care, to be strong, large, and handsome. In 754 robbers murdered Boniface while he was bringing the gospel to the Frisians, a tribe of pagans living to the north. A special crypt in the monastery still holds Boniface's bones today.

Besides the crypt that holds Boniface's bones, the basilica, a large church with a long sanctuary, was another important part of the abbey. It had two round, high towers pointing to the sky. Inside this sanctuary for worship the pillars and walls were decorated in a fine manner. Monks in the monastery in Fulda were specially trained in artistic accomplishments and other studies. The whole complex was an impressive sight to the travelers as they broke through the dense forests of Germany and saw the buildings ahead towering even higher than the trees.

The whole complex was an impressive sight to the travelers.

"Is that where I will live?" Gottschalk might have asked his father as they neared the monastery. "Yes, son, that is where you will live and learn and grow," he might have replied.

For Gottschalk it was a new and strange place to live. New and strange things happened here. During the oblation ceremony Gottschalk was led with his parents to the front of the sanctuary,

The music sung in the monasteries was called Gregorian chant, named after Pope Gregory the Great and developed during Charlemagne's lifetime. The songs were the monks' prayers sung all together, reverently, in a kind of wandering melody. Separate measures of rhythm in music had not been invented yet.

to the altar where the bread and wine were and where the priest stood when he performed the mass.[1] Gottschalk's parents then took his right hand and wrapped it in the altar cloth. They kissed his wrapped hand and gave it to the priest, symbolizing their offering of their son to God and to the church. Chanted prayers sung by a choir of monks in low, simple melody echoed between the high stone walls while the abbot, the head of the monastery, poured holy water onto the boy's head. Then the abbot shaved Gottschalk's head, leaving only a ring of hair around his bald scalp. That special haircut, called a tonsure, was a mark of being a monk.

Before the ceremony was even finished Gottschalk's parents were required to leave. Every reminder of Gottschalk's former life with them was taken away as well. The ceremony continued. The clothes he had on, probably an embroidered tunic and a pair of high stockings, were taken off him, and a loose black garment that hung down to his knees was put on him instead. Besides a few extra items, such as a handkerchief, belt, stockings, shoes, and a blanket and pillow for his bed, that was all Gottschalk was left with in the world.

The deed was done. Gottschalk was a monk. Vows to be a monk had been said, whether by Gottschalk's father or by Gottschalk himself as he was instructed to repeat the words. Final vows would come later when he was older. But for then Gottschalk was a member of the monastery in Fulda, with all its privileges and duties. Many, many duties.

Young Gottschalk became a monk.

CHAPTER 4

The monks in Fulda were called Benedictine monks. St. Benedict of Nursia had written a rulebook for monks several centuries earlier, and this rulebook was strictly followed and enforced at the monastery school in Fulda. Rabanus Maurus saw to that. He was a priest and the director of the school there. Soon he would become the abbot of the whole monastery in Fulda. Rabanus had been a part of the ceremony that brought Gottschalk into the Benedictine monastery as an oblate. That would, in fact, be an issue later on.

Rabanus was well educated. He had been taught at Charlemagne's palace school by the best teachers in the land, including the most famous instructor of that time, Alcuin. And Rabanus was no average teacher himself. Though he was not an original thinker, he was firm and well read, and he knew how to teach. Since the day Fulda was founded, it had very quickly become one of the most important monasteries around. That Rabanus was chosen as director of the school and then as the abbot was a testament to his abilities. In the areas of education, collecting books for the library, and holding of lands, Rabanus served the

An eighth-century copy of *St. Benedict's Rule.*

Talking while eating meals was strictly forbidden.

abbey in Fulda well, advancing it even more. He became known as the instructor of Germany.

Lack of strictness was becoming a problem in the empire, though. Not all monasteries were so primly and properly run. Even the rulers of the land, including Charlemagne and his son Louis the Pious, made decrees concerning the use of *St. Benedict's Rule* for monks. The *Rule* was considered a very important document in those days, and portions of it were supposed to be read in the monasteries every day. Rabanus was of the same mind. Rules and vows were important—very important.

What were some of those rules?

Besides one's necessary clothing, bedding, and very few personal items, including a handkerchief and a small knife (handy for sharpening quills when writing), the monks could own no other objects. The abbot was to regularly check all their beds "to see if any private property be found in them."[1] What would happen if the abbot found any extra possessions in someone's mattress? "Let him undergo the most severe discipline."[2]

"And let absolute silence be kept at table, so that no whispering may be heard nor any voice except the reader's."

—St. Benedict's Rule, "On the Weekly Reader"

16

Talking while eating meals was strictly forbidden. If someone wanted the salt or any other dish passed, he used sign language for his request.

There was no noisy clanking of silverware either. Forks were not in use at that time in history. Fingers were the main eating utensils, although spoons were used for eating soups and stews. But spoons were not heard scraping against bowls or plates either. Bowls were often made of bread—round loaves scooped out to form containers—and plates were made of rectangular, baked flat bread called trenchers. The trenchers and bread bowls were not always eaten, however. The custom was to give such food-soaked bread to the poor.

Meals in the monastery were not eaten in complete silence though. A passage of scripture or a portion from *St. Benedict's Rule* was read while the monks quietly ate their food.

And what would they eat? That was part of the *Rule* too. No

Dining rooms in monasteries were called refectories.

meat was allowed, unless one was sick and needed extra nourishment. No beef, lamb, pork, or venison would ever be brought in mouth-watering aroma to the refectory table. But vegetables, cheese, and eggs were offered in plenty—for one meal. Fish was permissible too. Each monk received a pound of bread every day.

No breakfast was offered. In early afternoon a large dinner was served. In addition to side dishes of fruits or vegetables and the bread, the monks could choose between two cooked, main dishes. A measured amount of wine and ale was available, although drinking water was encouraged. In summer when activity was greater and food more plentiful, a light supper was served in the evening.

> "Except the sick who are very weak, let all abstain entirely from eating the flesh of four-footed animals."
>
> —St. Benedict's Rule, "On the Measure of Food"

The routine of each day was extremely rigid and scheduled. The monks were required to rise at 3:00 a.m. for prayer and worship in the chapel. Then a little sleep, and another time of worship was required at sunrise in the chapel again. Back and forth, back and forth, at least seven times in a twenty-four-hour day every monk was required to attend prayer and worship. And woe to the young man who arrived late or who nodded off to nap at one of those services of prayer!

A full night's sleep never happened in a monastery. Never. No pajamas were needed. Each monk wore his monk's habit to bed so he wasted no time changing his clothes. An older, more experienced monk was assigned the task of watching over a younger one to make sure he followed all the rules. Monks slept together in one large, long room, each in his own slim bed. There was no place to hide—day or night.

The rules were many and harsh. But that was the idea. A monastery was a world apart from the world. One was there to try to get his mind off of this earth and to focus his whole attention on the things of heaven. This would be done primarily in prayer. Prayer was key to life in an abbey.

At least, that is what the monastery was supposed to be. But it still was a world within a world, even if it was another sort of one. When men entered the confining walls of a monastery, they left all their earthly possessions behind. Nevertheless, they took one very significant thing along with them into their new communal home: their sinful natures. Life was not perfect in a monastery. It never would be. Along with learning all the rules that governed the life of a monk, Gottschalk would discover that truth as well.

CHAPTER 5

Gottschalk received a fine education at the monastery school in Fulda. The director Rabanus Maurus demanded such an education for all his students. Thanks to Rabanus, the library in the school was well stocked with many books—as many as six hundred at one point. That was very, very many for those days. Rabanus had learned about the importance of books from his own teacher, Alcuin. With all those written works and Rabanus' scientific and religious knowledge, the young monks in Fulda could excel. It appears that Gottschalk did.

Gottschalk's family spoke an old type of German language. In Fulda Gottschalk learned to read and write Latin. Latin was the language of all educated persons of that day. He studied classical literature, poetry, theological writings of the church fathers, and the Bible—all in Latin. He learned to copy manuscripts, neatly drawing each letter with the quill of a feather that he must repeatedly dip into a small jar or horn of ink.

The students practiced writing by pressing marks into a tablet of wax, but they were finally trained to write on parchment. Parchment was expensive because it was made from animal hides. Paper was not available in Europe at that time. But there were advantages to writing on parchment. It was thicker than paper, so mistakes could be scraped off. Books of parchment also lasted very long. Parchment did not decay as paper did. Some of the more artistic students were trained to decorate letters or portions of the books they were copying, using colorful paints and inks. Fulda was known for its fine instruction in decorating books.

Copying books, letter by letter and word by word, was one of the main activities of monks in those days. Monasteries provided an important service to the world and to the church, because that was the only way that much of ancient writing was preserved. One book could easily be lost, but if more copies of that book had been faithfully reproduced, spare copies of the book would be available.

Because more and more copying was being done, language and rules for language began to develop and become clearer to people. Capitalization, punctuation, and spacing between words were new inventions at that time. People began to see

An example of medieval writing and decoration of that writing, called an illuminated manuscript.

how breaks between words and sentences were helpful to easily read what was written, even if they used more space on the costly

Copying manuscripts was one of the main tasks of monks in the Middle Ages. They worked in a room called a scriptorium.

21

parchment. Various monasteries began to develop their own style of handwriting. So did Fulda.

Copying manuscripts was an important service for education too. Schools needed math, science, and history books. The amount of available knowledge in all those subjects was not nearly as great as it is today. Much knowledge in science and math was yet to be discovered and much history was still to come. One person could know all there was to know in those subjects, which is certainly not possible today. Nevertheless, what was known then needed to be in books, and the printing press would not be invented for many centuries. In the meantime, everything must be copied by hand.

But the most important words the monks copied were those of scripture. One of their main tasks was also to make copies of the Holy Bible. And errors were not allowed in that work. It was a demanding task with much responsibility attached to it.

Gottschalk was trained in all this and more in Fulda. It was a busy life. A scheduled life.

Each monastery had a garden where the monks grew vegetables to eat and herbs for medicine. Such manual labor was part of the schedule too. Someone had to wash the clothes, cook the food, bake the bread, brew the ale, tend to the sick, and do whatever else was necessary for life to be self-sustaining inside the abbey.

Monks did every task. They took weekly turns doing chores such as serving the food and cleaning the kitchen after meals. Other jobs that required more expert knowledge, such as winemaking, were left to one monk who was "wise, of mature character, sober, not a great eater, not haughty."[1] In that case, that monk was called the cellarer. He was

"But as for coarse jests and idle words or words that move to laughter, these we condemn everywhere with a perpetual ban, and for such conversation we do not permit a disciple to open his mouth."

—St. Benedict's Rule, "On the Spirit of Silence"

also in charge of buying and preparing the food. No job was left unassigned.

Was there any time left for fun and games at all? We don't read of it. Outside the walls of the monastery children could laugh and run and play with their friends. Inside the walls all was solemn, serious, and quiet. Any young man behaving out of line with any of these rules was either beaten or forced to fast for a time. Not every boy was so suited to the strictness of monastic life.

Gottschalk began to wonder if he was one of those.

We do not know exactly when Gottschalk realized he did not want to be a monk, but it is not hard to imagine the thought entering the young man's head—especially when living as a monk had not been his own idea or choice. What is hard to imagine is that Gottschalk continued to think such thoughts and later tried to do something about it. Rabanus Maurus was known as a helpful and wise teacher, but he was also known for his deep convictions about strict rules in monasteries and firmly holding to one's vows. Vows were made never to be broken. That was what Gottschalk and all the oblates in Fulda had been taught. To be released from one's vows of being a monk was inexcusable, if not impossible, in Rabanus' thinking.

But Gottschalk was thinking too, and his thoughts were not running in the same direction as everyone else's. Yes, along with the other students in Fulda, he was excelling in his studies. Perhaps he was excelling too much for Rabanus' liking.

> *"With regard to boys and adolescents... whenever such as these are delinquent let them be subjected to severe fasts or brought to terms by harsh beatings, that they may be cured."*
>
> —St. Benedict's Rule, "How Boys are to Be Corrected"

CHAPTER 6

Fulda

Reichenau

ottschalk was growing and learning in Fulda. By the time he was in his teens, his gifts and talents were coming through. His teachers likely saw that he would benefit from the experience of being taught at another monastery school for a few years. It was common practice to send exceptionally bright students to other schools for a time.

Gottschalk was sent to a monastery in Reichenau (Rike-ĕ-naw), an island in a large lake just off the larger Lake Constance in southern Germany. A narrow strip of land led to the island

An aerial view of Reichenau today.

so Gottschalk did not have to ride a boat to get there, but it was indeed a place surrounded by water. In such a pleasant and refreshing area, cool breezes flowed freely off the lake onto the land. Rushes grew along the shoreline marshes. On the way Gottschalk heard the songs of the warblers, special birds suited in God's providence to life in those tall, broad grasses on the banks of the lake. We do not know if Gottschalk enjoyed the sounds and scenery there, however.

What was true of Fulda was true of this abbey as well: it was famous for its fine education, and the rules of monastic life were no less strictly observed. The sounds of deep male voices singing the wanderingly rhythmic and reverent songs of prayer throughout the day and night in Fulda also echoed among Reichenau's halls. The 3:00 a.m. abbey bell rang just as loudly in the misty island air as in the darkness of the river Fulda's shores. From that point of view, being at Reichenau was not much different than being at Fulda.

But being there still meant more changes for Gottschalk. He was away from Fulda and far away from German Saxony where

By the ninth century Reichenau was already well recognized as a center for monastic life. A number of monasteries and churches were built on the island, and several from that period in history still stand there.

he had been born. A poem he wrote in Latin seems to speak of his sadness. We do not know exactly why he wrote the poem, but some authors believe it describes his homesickness while he lived in the island monastery. One translation of the first verse of this famous poem reads as follows:

> Why do you bid me, little lad, me an exile far beyond
> the sea,
> to sing a sweet song? Oh, why do you bid me to sing?[1]

Another author translated the fifth verse of the poem this way:

> You know that the captive little people
> Called Israel
> Was ordered to sing
> In Babylon, far away
> From the bounds of Judah.
> O why are you telling me to sing?[2]

Despite the possibility of experiencing such downhearted feelings, Gottschalk met other helpful teachers in Reichenau as well as new friends. He met Walafrid Strabo there, a fellow student who was a little younger than himself. The two would be friends for life.

That Walafrid and Gottschalk became close friends proved significant later on, but that they enjoyed each other's company at first might seem unlikely. Walafrid was happy to be an oblate in a monastery, while Gottschalk was not. Walafrid would end up being a good friend of his next abbot, while Gottschalk would end up being an archenemy of that same man. Walafrid came from a poor family, while Gottschalk came from a rich and powerful one. However, both young men were able thinkers, both excelled in their studies, both liked to write poetry, and both liked to read what the church fathers had written.

Gottschalk especially liked to read about the doctrine of predestination. Walafrid even nicknamed his new friend Fulgentius after Fulgentius of Ruspe, a church father who, along with Augustine, had written much about the doctrine of predestination in centuries past. In fact, Walafrid had such a "high opinion of [Gottschalk's] learning and piety" that he wrote a poem for Gottschalk.[3] Walafrid was impressed by his friend's studious character and godly life. We can only imagine the conversations young Gottschalk and Walafrid had over what they were learning about poetry and doctrine. Such deep subjects were a good basis for fellowship.

That may seem strange to us. Friends today talk about many different things, some profound things and some silly things. But for young men and women who were secluded in monasteries and convents in those days, all they knew was whatever was taught to them in those places. Ancient writings of the church fathers and classical literature were what was important in those places. That is what the young men and women there knew. When allowed to talk, that is what they talked about. That was in the providence of God.

Gottschalk spent at least two years, or perhaps several more, at Reichenau and then was transferred back to Fulda. Walafrid was transferred there about the same time. Walafrid, as well as Gottschalk, was becoming a scholar in his own right. In fact, Walafrid would someday return to the island of Reichenau to be the abbot of the monastery there. For a number of years he would also be a chaplain of the empress and her young son, serving as the personal minister and priest of the emperor's family as well as tutoring the young prince. His talents would not leave him pulling weeds or copying manuscripts as a mere monk.

The teachers at Reichenau judged that Walafrid would benefit from learning under the famous and talented abbot of Fulda. So back north to Fulda both Gottschalk and Walafrid went. The journey was a welcome change of landscape from the constant confines of an abbey. Fulda was about 260 miles straight north of Reichenau, a sizable trip for the pair to make on foot. The boys were in their late teens or early twenties.

A new smaller church, the Church of St. Michael dedicated

The Church of St. Michael is one of the oldest churches still standing in Germany. A long hall and square tower were added to the church in 1092, and the height of both towers was raised in 1315, but other elements are as they were in Gottschalk's day.

to Michael the archangel, had recently been built in the cemetery next to the large basilica and other monastery buildings in Fulda. It was to be a chapel for the dead. Praying for deceased monks and other important families who had died and donated money to the monastery was a very important role of all monks in all monasteries. Some monasteries even traded names of dead monks so that monks in other monasteries could pray for their dead monks too. St. Michael's chapel might have been used for that purpose.

The construction started in 819, so Gottschalk probably saw the first stones laid before he left for Reichenau. When he returned to Fulda the chapel's arched, domed interior and its round tower pointing to the sky were finished. Monks from Fulda had worked on its construction and also added the decorations inside. All of the walls were painted with various scenes, including a representation of Michael the archangel and borders of various designs. The church was completed in 822, the same year that Rabanus Maurus was promoted from being director of the school in Fulda to being the abbot of the whole monastery. With only a few additions, the Church of St. Michael still stands today.

Before Gottschalk left for Reichenau, construction also began on some buildings that were being added to the large basilica that was part of the monastery. During a special ceremony the bones of St. Boniface were moved to a new altar in the western chancel of the church. Otherwise, the monastery, with its increasing importance in the government of the Roman Catholic Church, its two matching, majestic towers, and its scriptorium full of busy monks working with their colored inks, quills, parchments, and manuscripts, was all the same when he returned. Gottschalk heard the familiar ring of the bells. A river still gurgled nearby. The town that was beginning to spring up around the abbey was still growing.

A monk with the special job of porter greeted the young men and any others who were traveling with them as they approached the abbey. Gottschalk and Walafrid likely stepped together onto the rounded porch of the entrance to the monastery, and they likely were very glad for each other's company as they did so.

Very soon especially Gottschalk would need a good friend. Gottschalk would not fare so well under the new abbot of Fulda.

A porter was always ready to greet travelers.

CHAPTER 7

Gottschalk did not want to be a monk.

There is some reason to believe that his brothers or sisters urged him to protest against being one. We do not know Gottschalk's family situation in that regard, however. Perhaps Gottschalk was the firstborn and his siblings wanted him to get his inheritance back so that they could share in it. Gottschalk's father was a count, a wealthy and powerful man in the empire. When he and his wife gave Gottschalk and Gottschalk's inheritance to the monastery, that was a very large donation. But not everybody in Gottschalk's family agreed that was a good idea.

Gottschalk had arguments of his own, though, arguments that were not about land and money. He wanted his freedom. After he came back to Fulda from Reichenau around 826, he was of the age when an oblate was supposed to repeat and confirm his vows of being a monk. Instead, Gottschalk laid out his arguments against his being a monk and brought them to his abbot, Rabanus Maurus.

To be a monk was to be a slave. It was loss of freedom. Under Saxon law and tradition, two Saxon witnesses must be present if any Saxon was going to lose his freedom. Gottschalk was a Saxon— and there had not been two Saxon witnesses present when he was forced to become a monk. In fact, Gottschalk said that he had not chosen to be a monk, but that years ago Rabanus Maurus had forced Gottschalk as a child to become a monk.

Those were bold statements. Few men would dare say such things. Only four years earlier Rabanus Maurus had become the abbot of Fulda, and he was still establishing his position in the important and influential monastery there. He was firm in his beliefs and in discipline. Gottschalk had to have known that his arguments went against everything the abbot taught. There would be no sympathy from that man.

Indeed, there was not. In Rabanus' mind, a vow was a vow and an oblate was an oblate. These ought not be changed. These could not be changed. Even if a child or his parents made the vow, it was still a vow. And vows cannot be broken.

The battle lines were drawn.

Who would decide between the two? A synod must be called. The judgment would not be easy. Rabanus held a powerful and important position in the church. He "was by far the most influential churchman in the ninth century."[1] Men would listen to what he said. But Gottschalk's reasoning was logical and made sense. Some men in the church took Gottschalk's side as well. Besides, who would want to have monks in monasteries who did not want to be there? That would defeat the purpose. Even the future abbot of Fulda, the man who would later replace Rabanus, sided with Gottschalk. No, it would not be an easy decision.

It was June of 829. Summer was just beginning, and a synod was held at Mainz, about 95 miles southwest of Fulda. Rabanus Maurus, young Gottschalk, and other leading men in the church were there. Perhaps Gottschalk's relatives were there too. Rabanus stated his arguments. Gottschalk stated his. The synod voted and ended with a compromise. Neither side won. The synod judged that Gottschalk did not have to be a monk anymore. He was free, but his inheritance must stay with the church. Rabanus was unhappy. Gottschalk's relatives were not happy either.

Gottschalk returned to Fulda. He could pack his belongings— his very few belongings—and leave. It would not take long.

Rabanus returned to Fulda as well. He was packing too, but not belongings. He was packing thoughts. *Gottschalk did not have to keep his vow to be a monk.* That went against everything Rabanus thought and believed. That endangered the whole system of monastic life. Besides, that left Rabanus looking rather foolish. He, an important abbot of an important monastery, said the vow must be kept. One young monk said he did not have to keep his vow, and a synod had agreed. The decision made at Mainz could not be allowed to stand.

Yes, the battle lines were drawn. Rabanus was on one side and Gottschalk was on the other. The war was just begun.

Rabanus was on one side and Gottschalk was on the other.

CHAPTER 8

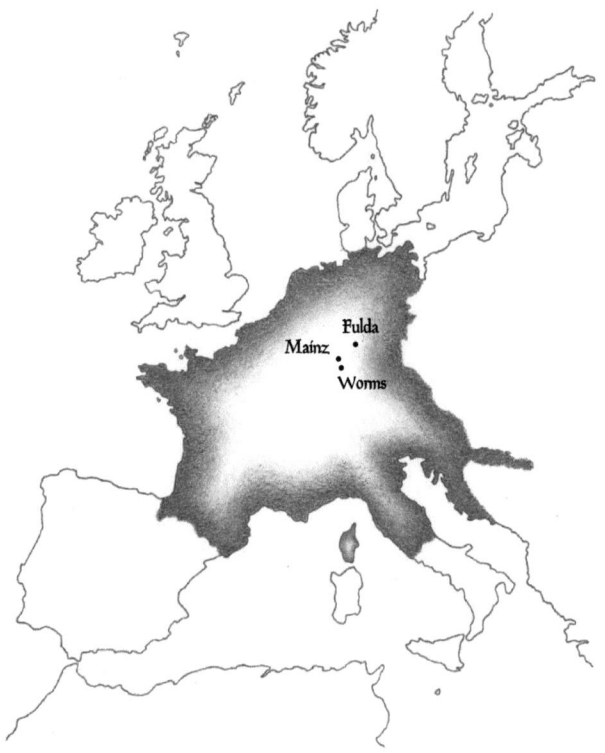

Maínz   Fulda
    •
    •
  Worms

abanus had a plan. He got busy. He called for another synod to hear the case and invited Emperor Louis the Pious to be the president to lead. Rabanus was friends with the emperor. They thought alike on matters of strict living in monasteries, and Louis had ruled about that before. Rabanus likely thought, *Surely Louis will take my side. And what the emperor said will be law—especially if he was in charge of the whole assembly.* The synod was scheduled to take place at Worms (Vorms) in August, two months later.

Rabanus also wrote a detailed treatise entitled *On the Oblation of Children*. It was a document directed squarely against Gottschalk. Rabanus said that monks and oblates may never break their vows, because keeping their vows was a matter of faith.

Rabanus was also concerned that the church could lose a rich inheritance like Gottschalk's. Especially the abbey at Fulda had become rich in lands, power, and wealth from such donations. *Very* rich and powerful. Such wealth and power could be in jeopardy if monks broke their vows.

Besides, the Franks had conquered the Saxons, so Saxon law and tradition did not count anymore. Therefore, Gottschalk's argument that his childhood vows had to be witnessed by two legal Saxons did not hold.

"The monastery of Luxeuil had in the 9th century an estate with 15,000 farm-houses upon it."[1]

If all this was not enough, Rabanus had one more point to argue, a point that perhaps angered him the most. Gottschalk had said that to be a monk is to lose one's freedom. It is slavery. And in the case of an oblate, it is forced slavery. Rabanus wanted to counter that statement especially. Yes, to be a monk is to be a slave, Rabanus said, but that is a good thing. "The holy fathers deemed it a great honor to be called slaves of God," he wrote in his treatise.[2]

Among other grievous descriptions, Rabanus wrote of those who were "ungrateful," those who were "heretics," and also referred to Gottschalk as "this our adversary."[3] Heretics are especially terrible people. Heretics teach lies. Rabanus' opinion of the young monk was clear. Gottschalk was on enemy ground.

With these arguments Rabanus, along with a number of other high-ranking bishops, came to the Synod of Worms. Emperor Louis the Pious came as well. Gottschalk was only in his twenties as he was surrounded by those older men in their fine robes, Rabanus' golden crozier, and the emperor's jeweled crown. The

Gottschalk was only in his twenties as he was surrounded by many older men at the synod.

high, vaulted ceilings, arches, and carved work within the cathedral where they met complimented the status and position of Abbot Rabanus Maurus, his emperor friend, and the other men there. The lofty walls and royal finery contrasted with the plainness of young Gottschalk, who wore his rough, dark monk's habit as he stood before those mighty dignitaries to defend his position of not wanting to be a monk.

Would Gottschalk keep his freedom? Or would he have to keep his head shaved in a tonsure, wear his rough, hooded robe, and claim the cloister for his home?

No one knows for sure what happened at that synod. The records are lost. Most historians assume that Gottschalk lost his case. His inheritance still belonged to the church, and so did he. Gottschalk must remain a monk. However, Gottschalk was not required to return to Fulda. He would not have to see Rabanus every day, and Rabanus would not have to look into the eyes of his adversary every day. We can imagine such a decision was a relief to both of them.

Instead, Gottschalk was allowed to travel to at least two other mon-

The staff that an abbot, bishop, or pope holds in ceremony is called a crozier, symbolizing his office as shepherd of a flock. This one is from the thirteenth century.

Cloister is another word for abbey, monastery, or convent, but it also refers to the long, covered porch of the courtyard of an abbey.

asteries before he joined the monastery of Orbais in France. To history he would be known as Gottschalk of Orbais because he would say his final monastic vows there.

That Gottschalk was not required to return to Fulda was unusual. Student monks could switch monastery schools for a time for the sake of education, but to change monasteries as an adult monk was forbidden. Monks must stay in the monastery where they joined. A few exceptions such as doing missionary work might be considered, or traveling to fetch or trade manuscripts might be a necessary errand, but the general rule was that a monk may never leave his monastery, and certainly he may never leave without permission.

The abbot even screened monks' letters from their families, and their visits were not welcomed.

Gottschalk did not get his inheritance back and never would. But there was one thing he could not lose: the education he had received. He had a remarkable memory, and what he had learned would not be lost.

"From memory, he could recite passages from the church fathers throughout a whole day without any break."[4]

37

Gottschalk visited other monasteries to continue his studies under various instructors and to benefit from the books that their libraries held. He met new people and gained new friends in those places. He especially would look into the writings of Augustine while at Orbais.

Gottschalk also gained valuable experience at Worms. How did it come about that a monk in his twenties would be required to stand and make his case before some of the most important men in the whole world? Why would world rulers and other powerful men in the church care about one plain young man?

The whole system of monastic life was at stake. If one oblate was allowed to forsake his vows and leave his monastery, more monks might follow. From the church's viewpoint maintaining strict rules in the monasteries was difficult enough without the possibility of monastic vows being broken. On a few occasions others had tried to escape these vows, but it is doubtful whether any of them had such clearness of mind to argue the point as this young man did. Gottschalk's case could cause trouble. He was only one monk, but he was a bold and logical one, with rich and powerful relatives.

Whether Gottschalk's arguments prevailed or not, in the providence of God the experience served him well. He would stand before bishops and rulers again, when other matters of even greater weight must be decided. Matters of unfathomable weight.

CHAPTER 9

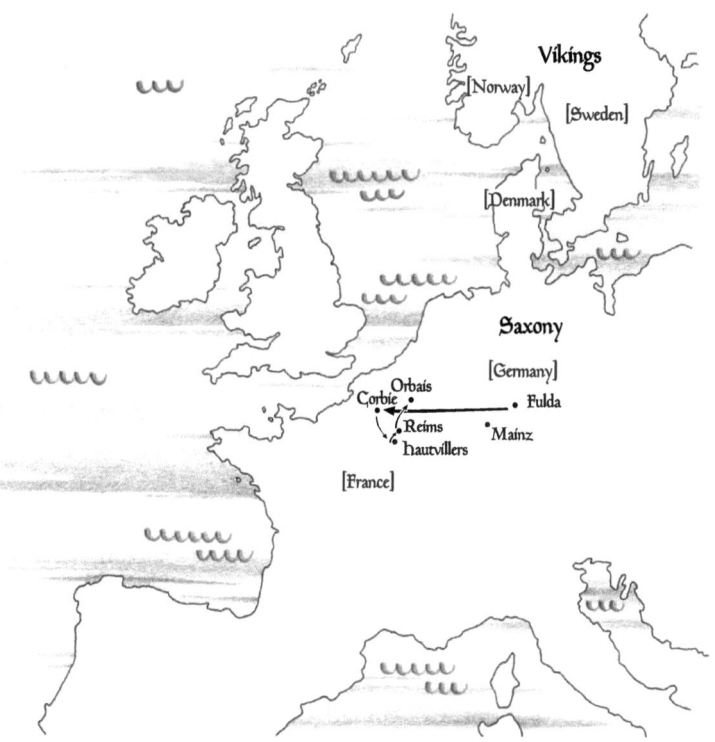

Gottschalk did not go to Orbais immediately. He spent time at the monastery in Corbie (Keer-bee), as well as at the abbey in Hautvillers (Oat-vill-yā). He also stayed for a while in the home of Ebbo, the archbishop of Reims (Rĕm), and his visit with Ebbo was of no little significance. The archbishop of Reims held one of the most powerful positions in France. In all these places Gottschalk gained more friends and continued his studies in doctrine and poetry. Some of Gottschalk's poetry, considered by many to be some of the best verse written in the medieval age, dates from that time.

This artwork is contained in a decorated copy of the Bible known as the Ebbo Gospels. It also contains a dedication poem that scholars believe was written by Gottschalk.

Among others, the monks Rimbert and Ratramnus were two more contacts Gottschalk made. He might have already known Ratramnus from Reichenau. These monks lived at Corbie, and Gottschalk discussed predestination with them. Both agreed with Gottschalk's views of predestination. Ratramnus and Gottschalk later exchanged letters written in pure and beautiful poetic lines rather than in usual prose. Ratramnus also later tried to defend Gottschalk's views on predestination before the king of France. Gottschalk was strengthening many important friendships at this time in his life.

Exactly why Gottschalk finally joined Orbais as a monk and confirmed his vows there, we do not know. He did so willingly. Perhaps he did this in submission to the decision reached at the Synod of Worms. That is most likely. Perhaps he had few choices left. Even if he had been freed from his vow, without his inheritance he had no income. He had to do something. He was a scholar, and he was fast becoming a theologian. If he wanted to continue these studies, he had to be where books were, and books were in monasteries.

Besides these possibilities, perhaps the political turmoil of the day was behind his entering Orbais. The three sons of Emperor Louis the Pious had been fighting among themselves and even against their father. Ebbo, the archbishop with whom Gottschalk had stayed, had taken the side of the oldest son against his father. Shortly thereafter their father the emperor was in full power again. He deposed Ebbo from office and imprisoned him. All this happened in 835. Ebbo was no longer welcomed as an archbishop

Gottschalk joined the monastery in Orbais, a small town
in north central France. An ancient abbey still stands there,
although it has been rebuilt since Gottschalk's day.

in Louis' realm. Nor was it a good time to be seen as Ebbo's friend.
Joining Orbais would set Gottschalk apart from this man.

Safety from the danger of Viking raids was not a reason for
Gottschalk to enter Orbais, however. Viking raids at this time were
a constant threat, especially in summer when those merciless men
paddled their longboats down from Denmark, Norway, and Sweden
up into the rivers of western Europe to any farms, towns, or villages
along the banks. The more successes they enjoyed, the more they
marched inland from the rivers to plunder, steal, and kill. Monasteries
were one of their favorite targets. The Frankish kingdom in the 830s
was not a very stable or safe place to be—not anywhere.

For whatever reasons, Gottschalk joined the monastery
of Orbais that was nestled in the wooded hills of northeastern

France. The monastery had about ninety monks at that time, and while Gottschalk was there he busied himself in studying the writings of Augustine. His passion was the doctrine of double predestination. Perhaps he thought, *If I must be a monk, studying Augustine will make it worthwhile.*

His interest in that doctrine might have seemed strange and new to people back then. It is still strange to many people today. But history would prove it was not strange at all. Nor was it new. The doctrine of double predestination would be key to the Reformation's sounding forth of the truth of the gospel in the sixteenth century. It would be key to the Synod of Dordt's eloquent answer to the Arminians in the seventeenth century.

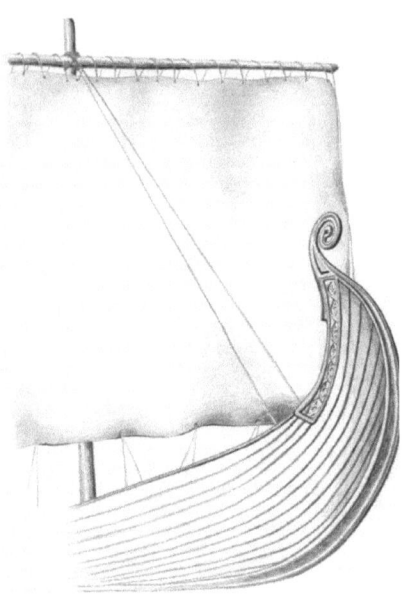

Viking raids at this time were a constant threat.

The truth of scripture does not change. The doctrine of election and reprobation was key in Gottschalk's day. The doctrine was key in Augustine's day. The doctrine was key from the beginning of time.

"And I will put enmity between thee and the woman, and between thy seed and her seed; it shall bruise thy head, and thou shalt bruise his heel" (Gen. 3:15). These words were spoken by God to the devil in the garden of Eden, drawing an impassable line of spiritual warfare between all the reprobate seed of the serpent and all the elect seed of the woman, of which Jesus Christ is *the* elect, *the* coming seed of the woman: "And to thy seed, which is Christ" (Gal. 3:16).

Without election and reprobation, we cannot understand the sovereignty of God in salvation. Without election and reprobation, we cannot understand who God is at all.[1]

How was it that Gottschalk understood these things, seemingly all alone, while other theologians in his day talked about predestination as well? The doctrine was not unknown. God did not allow his truth to be completely forgotten in those dark ages of history. His church must continue to exist in the world throughout all of time. The truth was there, but it was not always so clear. Gottschalk wanted to be clear.

The Spirit must continue to lead the church of Christ to understand the truth more and more. "He will guide you into all truth" (John 16:13). That can be the only explanation for Gottschalk's desire. That is why Gottschalk understood these truths to the degree that he did. That is why he could put these truths and doctrines together in ways that other theologians of his time, though they confessed predestination too, could not. Gottschalk saw how election and reprobation fit into the truth of salvation and how confessing that truth gives all the glory to the almighty and unchanging God. That is a gift of the Holy Spirit. A gift of grace.

Gottschalk was glad to give witness to the wonderful truths God was bringing him to see and to learn in scripture and in the writings of Augustine and other church fathers. His fellow monks in Orbais heard the excitement in his voice. They were well aware of Gottschalk and the doctrines about which he spoke. When he pointed those things out to them, they understood them too. Yes, the doctrine of election and reprobation made sense. It was logical. It was in scripture. It was beautiful.

Not everyone would see it that way, however.

CHAPTER 10

In his late twenties and into his early thirties, Gottschalk studied election and reprobation and spoke of it wherever he went. All his friends knew what was on this young man's mind: doctrine. And double predestination was at the heart of it. Especially while at Orbais he further studied Augustine's writings on the doctrine. Gottschalk could show the truth of it from scripture and from the church fathers. And his arguments were convincing.

Why were his arguments so convincing? Why did they have to be convincing at all if the church already taught predestination, the doctrine is found in the Bible, and respected church fathers like Augustine had taught it long ago?

Why then? Because the doctrine of election and reprobation, when strictly and properly explained, gives all the glory for salvation to God. If man wants to have any glory in salvation for himself, man is robbed of it by predestination.

Salvation starts in election—election from all eternity—and the choice has nothing whatsoever to do with the works of men in time. Their good works are, in fact, the evidence of their election and the result of their election. Their good works come from God as a gift from him. God does not look into the future to see who will be good and who will be bad and then decide who will be elect and who will be reprobate. The future does not determine election. Election determines the future.

Who gets the credit for doing good works then? God gives good works to us to do, and we do them out of thanks. He gives them to us because he elected us to do them. "We are his workmanship, created in Christ Jesus unto good works, which God hath before ordained that we should walk in them" (Eph. 2:10). Therefore, God gets all the glory.

Just as a teabag is steeped in a kettle of steaming hot water, the Roman Catholic Church by that time in history was already steeped in the teaching of man's own merit for doing good works. Man must earn his salvation, at least in part. The whole monastic lifestyle was wrapped up in that idea. If a man joined a monastery, he earned some merit for doing that good work. He went above and beyond the normal call of duty for a Christian. He did something extra. God surely would want to bring him to heaven then. Why? Because he was such a good person! The idea of earning such a reward from God brought lots of men and their money into the church. This "tea" of merit was already quite dark by the 800s.

How could this happen? Although the truth of election and reprobation could not be denied, it was not a developed doctrine, nor a welcome doctrine. Theologians in Gottschalk's day spoke of predestination and man's inability to save himself. Alcuin had been one such man. But other theologians spoke of the ability of man partly to save himself. One can find writings explaining salvation both ways, so the doctrine was unclear.

In addition, the whole monastic system would be undermined and destroyed if a firm grasp of the truth of election and reprobation were to be taught and confessed. From the church's viewpoint that could not be allowed to happen at that late date in history. Monasteries had already been in existence for hundreds of years. Monasticism was an accepted way of life.

Double predestination was an unwelcome doctrine to those who strongly believed in the rules and ways of the Roman Catholic Church. If election is true, you go to heaven because God chose you to go there—not because you decided it or because you did enough or because you became a model monk or nun. And if election is true, God will work it all out in Jesus Christ to make sure you, as an elect child of God, will get to heaven. The glory for doing it is God's alone. There is no glory for monks or nuns or anybody else in that.

So Gottschalk had much convincing to do.[1] He began with his friends in the monasteries. That God alone receives all the glory was a beautiful thing to Gottschalk. He saw it as the truth, as precious, glorious truth, and he did not want to hide something so wonderful as that. Even as we might discover a new and beautiful insect or flower that we have never seen before and call our friends over to examine it with us, so Gottschalk showed the truth he had discovered to everyone he met.

We do not have recorded the exact words that Gottschalk said to convince his fellow monks at Orbais, but we do have a record of many words he wrote later in his life. He may have used some of those same words at this time. He wrote the following as a prayer, but the prayer explains what he believed. His explanation begins with who God is.

> Therefore, because Thou, Lord, alone art who Thou art (Ex. 3:4), even as Thou Thyself has testified; and as David likewise says to Thee: "Thou Thyself art forever the same" (Ps. 102:27)...it is manifest very clearly; and should be clear to anyone of sober wisdom, that Thou hast foreknown and predestinated already, before the ages.[2]

God is "forever the same." He does not change. Therefore, he decides who are elect and who are reprobate "before the ages," outside of time. Things in time can change, but God does not.

Gottschalk was always careful to prove all his arguments from scripture. Thus other fellow monks in Orbais, perhaps many of them, believed the truths he spoke. It is possible that the abbot, the head of the monastery, did as well.

Gottschalk was ordained to be a priest while he was in Orbais.

Gottschalk was ordained to be a priest while he was in Orbais. As a priest he could preach and teach these things even more. And as a priest it was possible for him to leave the monastery in Orbais to be a missionary and to proclaim these truths elsewhere.

Later there would be some question about his ordination as a priest. The bishop who had charge over the area surrounding Orbais was supposed to ordain the priests, but only the chorbishop, an assistant bishop, had been available to ordain Gottschalk. Someday that fact would be used against Gottschalk.

In the meantime, the fact was that Gottschalk was a priest, and he could labor as a priest. He could be a missionary and preach. In the providence and counsel of God, the witness of the truth of double predestination would spread.

CHAPTER 11

The monastery in Corbie, north of Orbais, served as a base for monks as they ventured north to the pagan Scandinavians, bringing the gospel to them in the light of the truth of predestination. Rimbert, one of the monks whom Gottschalk had met earlier, was one of them.

Gottschalk left the monastery of Orbais around the year 836 to travel south toward Italy and to many places throughout the southeastern part of the Holy Roman Empire. He was not traveling for pleasure. In these politically dangerous times travel was unsafe. The sons of the emperor, Louis the Pious, were grown, and they were constantly quarreling among themselves for power.

Protecting pilgrims and other wayfarers was not a great concern of rulers at that time.

Nor was traveling quick and easy. Gottschalk traveled some 620 miles, probably on foot. Benedictine monks took vows of poverty, so if he rode a horse or a mule, it was not one he owned. And he had to cross the Alps or go around them to get to Italy.

It was not easy traveling. But he traveled for good reason: to spread the gospel, and at the heart of that gospel was the doctrine of election and reprobation. He proclaimed that message in every area he went, bringing with it the comfort that flows from that doctrine. He preached to as many people as possible for the next ten years of his life. Wherever he went he was recognized as an important and prominent preacher of predestination.

Gottschalk went to the regions of Italy, Austria, Bavaria, Caesarea, Constantinople, Croatia, and more. His labors were wide and numerous. The significance and importance of his activities for the spiritual awakening and growth of the church of Jesus Christ cannot be underestimated. By the preaching, God is pleased to gather and defend his church and to build her up in grace, faith, and truth. It is not for us to know the effect of Gottschalk's preaching on the church of that day, but we can be sure if it was true preaching of the word of God, it had a great effect.

Based on the writings of Gottschalk, the judgment can be made that what this Benedictine monk preached was indeed the truth. He taught the unchangeableness of a sovereign, all-powerful God. That is where he started: God is immutable. And if God does not change, God's choice in eternity of who is elect and who is not is determined by him alone. That choice remains the same. Man cannot change God's choice in time. Many centuries later Calvinism called this doctrine *unconditional election*.

Election in eternity does not depend on what men do or do not do after they are born and living their lives. That is a very comforting doctrine. How so? Because it means that no elect can possibly go lost. God will not allow it. What he determines to happen will happen. He is God.

Gottschalk saw another doctrine too. If God predestined some to be reprobate, why would Christ die for them? The answer is that he did not die for them. The reformers of the sixteenth century called this doctrine *limited atonement*. Christ died only for the elect. Gottschalk taught that doctrine.[1]

In Gottschalk's *Tome to Gislemar* where Gottschalk explained how Christ died only for the elect, he wrote, "And so it is seen quite clearly that no one who has been redeemed by the blood of your [Christ's] cross ever perishes."[2] Christ died only for the elect, and that work surely does what it was supposed to do. It saves them.

If Christ died for all men and some men nevertheless go to hell, then God failed. He did not accomplish everything he wanted to. What a terrible thought that was for Gottschalk! No, that could not be. Election is certain. God does not change. Christ died only for the elect, and all the elect will surely go to heaven. God accomplishes whatever he purposes. Of that, Gottschalk had no doubt. That is what Gottschalk preached.[3]

All these truths fit together. If one doctrine is true, the other is true also, and so on. Gottschalk understood the logic of scripture. That was one of the main things that set him apart from other preachers of his day. Gottschalk was logical not for the sake of being logical, however. He saw the flow of the truth in scripture, like a river that must inevitably rush into the mighty waves of the ocean. There is no stopping it. Zeal for the truth of the word of God burned in his soul. Seeing the truth in scripture was first.

But something more set Gottschalk apart from other men. He was a gifted man. His poetry and his letters to leading theologians prove that. In thinking ability he was their equal. More than understanding the truth, therefore, more, even, than being zealous for the truth set Gottschalk apart.

Why is special note taken of him in history? Why would he be singled out later in his life to be tried by councils and synods for what he taught, even while other men taught similar things? It was because God gave Gottschalk the clearness of mind to understand the scriptures for what they taught in all their truth, without being clouded by the faulty traditions of men that were already creeping over the church like a thick and dangerous fog. Gottschalk saw through the fog. And he wasn't afraid to say so.

That set him apart from other men. He did not consider the consequences. Only the truth mattered to him. Zeal for the truth is one thing. To maintain zeal for the truth in the face of opposition is another. Gottschalk was given both.

There can be no doubt that Gottschalk's preaching had an effect. The courage he would exhibit later in his life to maintain the truth he taught and confessed would be astounding. His courage to bring the truth to many people throughout the lower regions of the Frankish empire we can be sure was in that same vein. Preaching is tremendously important, for "how shall they hear without a preacher?" (Rom. 10:14).

As Gottschalk went from city to city and town to town, a trumpet blast of the preached word roared in those regions of the empire. He was a master of words, and he had a memory to match. He knew how to expound and explain the doctrines of scripture to people who had never heard such things before.

"Hincmar implied in that...letter, that as a teacher Gottschalk was a master with words and quite convincing to his hearers."[4]

Toward the end of his missionary tour, between 846 and 848, Gottschalk traveled to Croatia, an area of the Mediterranean coastline in the far southeast of the empire. While he was there he saw an important battle, and his presence in that place at that time had some political significance. He may have been an interpreter between the two sides. The country of Croatia still remembers Gottschalk's role concerning his witness

1996 Croatian stamp that features Gottschalk.

of this event. A Croatian postage stamp commemorating Gottschalk was issued in 1996.

Many details of all these events are unknown, however. It seems a young man accompanied him on his journey through this region, but whether the young man was a friend or a nephew is uncertain. In one of Gottschalk's writings he called this companion "my little son."[5]

Evidence of Gottschalk's missionary work can nevertheless be seen in Croatia. It is possible that he was responsible for building a church there. Still standing today is a small church with an inscription over the door containing Gottschalk's name. If this is so, establishing that chapel was one of the last things Gottschalk did while he was still a free man.

The Holy Cross Chapel at Nin, the church in Croatia that Gottschalk might have built.

CHAPTER 12

Gottschalk preached throughout southeastern Europe for approximately ten years, but that is not all there is to the history. While he proclaimed his message of double predestination and the other truths of grace implied in that doctrine, his home base was in northern Italy at the estate of Eberhard, the margrave of Frioul (Free-EWL). Frioul was the area of northeastern Italy that Charlemagne had conquered and added to the Frankish kingdom.

Eberhard was not a king or a prince, but he was close to that. Eberhard had married Gisela, a daughter of Louis the Pious and a granddaughter of Charlemagne. That made Eberhard son-in-law to the emperor and a brother-in-law to all those sons of the emperor who were constantly fighting among themselves for more territory, and who were even fighting against their father in their vicious greed for power. The whole empire was a dangerous place to be, not only because anyone could be caught up in these bloody struggles between the royal brothers, but also because all those rulers were attending to their own fortunes and not so much to the threat of Viking raids and other invaders. They provided little protection to the citizens

Margrave is a rank above count but below prince or duke. The job of the margrave was to be the military commander of the region over which he was assigned, to protect the borders of the empire in that area.

of their Frankish kingdom, and the ferocious Vikings were taking advantage of the situation.

But Gottschalk was living in a relatively safe place in the empire with Eberhard, his wife, and their eight children. How was that? The sons of Louis the Pious, although they were fighting among themselves, all respected Eberhard. That put him in a unique and important position in the kingdom. He would play a special role concerning these princes, helping them to finally come to an agreement by making the Treaty of Verdun in 843.

This treaty successfully settled the territory each brother would rule. It was a significant event in the history of Europe that began to establish the boundary lines of the countries we know as France and Germany today. But it did not solve all the empire's problems. Vikings still raided what was left of any towns or villages, and not much was left. They soon attacked bigger cities like Paris. Nevertheless, the treaty helped to bring some peace to the kingdom, and progress was made. All this was going on while Gottschalk was preaching in and around Eberhard's territory of northern Italy.

How did Gottschalk come to stay by Eberhard and Gisela? Did these important, royal people simply take in wandering monks and priests? Probably not. Although it was common practice for nobles to give meals and lodging to traveling clergymen as they were doing errands for the church, and visiting clergymen were indeed welcome guests in any castle they came to, the stay of Gottschalk with the margrave and his family was more significant than that. Gottschalk was not merely passing through.

There might have been a connection with Walafrid Strabo, the longtime faithful friend of Gottschalk who not only was destined to be the abbot of Reichenau, but also was well acquainted with Eberhard's in-law relatives. Walafrid had been the personal chaplain to minister to the spiritual needs of Queen Judith, Gisela's mother. Walafrid had also been a tutor to Gisela's brother, later known as

Charles the Bald. So Walafrid was close to the royal family and was loved by them. It is possible that Walafrid arranged for Gottschalk to stay with them. Since Eberhard and his wife were known as very religious people, they likely would not have shied away from giving hospitality, even extended hospitality, to a missionary.

We do not know how long Gottschalk stayed in Eberhard's magnificent castle, situated in the midst of a section of prime farmland between the Mediterranean and the Alps. It was a pleasant place to stay. Gottschalk was comfortable in the luxurious surroundings and royal manners, for he had been born into a count's family, the rank just under that of margrave. But Gottschalk likely also remained under the margrave's care and protection while he went about the neighboring regions to preach and teach. We know that Eberhard and his wife, Gisela, welcomed Gottschalk into their castle and fellowship and provided for his needs and for those of any companions he had with him.

Gottschalk no doubt brought the message of the gospel to his royal hosts. In Gottschalk's zeal they likely were some of the first to hear his explanations of predestination and grace. However, we do not know if they embraced his teaching and believed it. There is no record.

One day a letter arrived.

In the providence of God, Gottschalk was safe while he labored to bring the true gospel of God's unchanging grace and double predestination throughout the southern part of the realm. In ten years' time many people heard these truths explained, and many people rejoiced with Gottschalk to know and understand these truths more. But also in the providence of God, Gottschalk's safety lasted only so long. Not everybody rejoiced to hear the truth. His safety lasted until one day a letter arrived, addressed to the margrave of Frioul.

CHAPTER 13

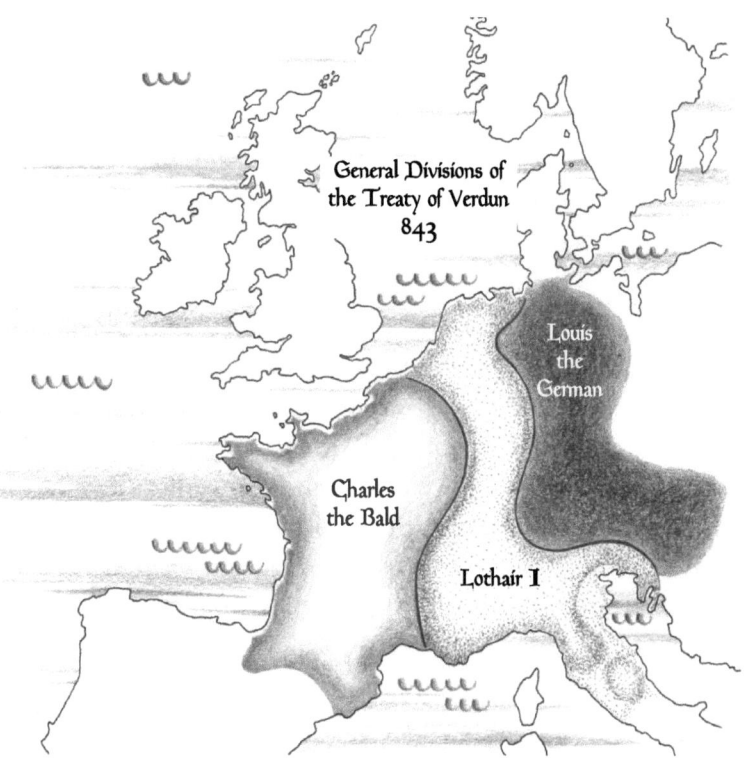

General Divisions of
the Treaty of Verdun
843

Louis
the
German

Charles
the Bald

Lothair I

Many people believe the truth when it is preached. Some do not. That is always the case when the word of God is proclaimed. The word is a sword. Scripture tells us that the word is a "savour of death unto death" and a "savour of life unto life" (2 Cor. 2:16). It is a *two*-edged sword. Some people love the gospel. Some people hate it. That ought not surprise us. Jesus said to his disciples, "If the world hate you, ye know that it hated me before it hated you" (John 15:18).

A bishop who lived in Brescia, an ancient Roman city in the

province of Verona in northwestern Italy just below the Alps, heard what Gottschalk was preaching and did not like it. Gottschalk had come to Brescia to preach and to meet with the bishop. His name was Bishop Noting or Notingus. He was a powerful man who in a few years would be known not only as bishop but also as count.

Already by May of 840 Bishop Noting of Verona talked about what the traveling preacher from Orbais was proclaiming in his province. The bishop heard that the renowned Rabanus Maurus, the current abbot of Fulda, was passing through the area. Noting went to meet with the abbot to alert him to what Gottschalk was teaching. If Noting knew Rabanus and expected Rabanus to side with him against Gottschalk, he was right. Rabanus had a ready ear. After the meeting Rabanus wrote a letter to Noting and described what he and Noting had spoken of together as "a heresy that some people are wickedly defending concerning the predestination of God."[1] Rabanus and Noting already used the word *heresy* in connection with Gottschalk.

Along with this letter to Noting, Rabanus included another letter about predestination. Rabanus wrote this document against Gottschalk's teaching on election and reprobation, although Rabanus did not name Gottschalk in it. Rabanus explained his arguments from scripture and the church fathers to try to prove that Gottschalk's teaching about predestination was wrong. Bishop Noting had asked Rabanus to write these arguments, and it appears that Rabanus wasted no time in doing that. Noting wanted to show the letter to the people in his province and try to convince them that Gottschalk's teachings were false.

There is little doubt that Rabanus intended to do something more at this time than write letters about Gottschalk. If he had, that might have cut Gottschalk's teaching in and around Italy in half. But suddenly Rabanus was too busy to worry about Gottschalk. The turmoil in the empire caused by the quarreling sons of Louis the Pious affected Rabanus. Rabanus had been a strong supporter and friend of Emperor Louis the Pious in all of these conflicts. In fact, when Rabanus was passing through near Noting's province, he was traveling in the company of the emperor.

Shortly after that, in June of 840, Louis the Pious died.

Rabanus had to choose which son of Louis he would support to rule the empire. He chose the oldest son, Lothair. This proved to be a poor choice. One of the younger sons, Louis the German, conquered his older brother and came into power instead. Rabanus had not been friendly with this younger son.

Until the political situation would change, Rabanus left the monastery in Fulda to go elsewhere to quietly study and write. A man named Hatto became the new abbot of Fulda. For the time being Rabanus was not in a position to deal with any church matters. When the power of both church and state are wrapped in each other, troubles in the state mean troubles in the church too. That was happening.

But Rabanus' exile was only for a short time. The political situation in Europe settled down with the Treaty of Verdun in 843. It would take a few more years, but the situation for Rabanus would change too. He had been one of the most highly respected and educated leaders in the church. In this empire where too few men could read and write, education was highly prized. Rabanus wrote a scholarly work called a grammar, a textbook about language and the scientific knowledge known up to that point in time. He also wrote a commentary on the book of Ezekiel, among others. Louis the German would not forget such a valuable man.

In 845 Rabanus was given an even higher position in the church. He became archbishop of Mainz, a position in which he was over many bishops, priests, and churches in Germany. He lived in Mainz and became a leader in the church in the large, grand cathedral there. The new emperor, Louis the German, had even urged Rabanus to take this post.

Rabanus was an intelligent man with a good memory. He did

not forget the earlier conversation between himself and Bishop Noting concerning Gottschalk. Certainly, he did not forget Gottschalk, the young monk, then grown, whom Rabanus had called "this our adversary" almost twenty years earlier. Rabanus was in a position in 846 to track Gottschalk down, and that would not be hard to do. Gottschalk was not trying to hide.

Rabanus, the new archbishop of Mainz wrote a letter to Eberhard, margrave of Frioul. Had not Rabanus been good friends with Eberhard's father-in-law, Louis the Pious, while the emperor was alive? Rabanus was even a friend of Eberhard, as previously they had exchanged letters. Eberhard had questions. Perhaps he did not know what terrible things that missionary Gottschalk was teaching, that wandering monk who was dwelling under the margrave's own roof. Rabanus would inform Eberhard of the details.

CHAPTER 14

Rabanus' letter to Eberhard was sharp and to the point.

They say that a certain know-it-all named Gottschalk is staying with you, who is teaching that the predestination of God binds all men...Therefore I have written these things to you, dearest friend, that you may know the sort of scandal that this opinion...has generated in this people and that, if anyone staying with you is impudently teaching things that are contrary to the correct faith, you may forbid him so that he desists from this sect.[1]

Rabanus told Eberhard to make Gottschalk stop teaching things "contrary to the correct faith." What he was teaching was shameless and disrespectful, Rabanus said. Rabanus called Gottschalk names and a leader of a sect—a serious charge because a sect is not the true church, but a group of people following a leader. Rabanus also exaggerated Gottschalk's teaching and preaching about predestination to make it appear sinful and wrong. In a word, Rabanus lied about it. That is a strong statement, but there are historical reasons and scriptural reasons to claim that was a lie.

What did Rabanus say that must be judged as false? He accused Gottschalk with the same terrible arguments with which God's people have been accused throughout all time. The apostle Paul dealt with them. The reformers would deal with them again and again. One can hear the same arguments today. They are this: your doctrine makes men careless and profane, meaning your doctrine makes men live unholy lives and makes those who believe it not to try to do good works. It makes men say, "Shall we continue in sin, that grace may abound?" (Rom. 6:1).

If you teach that God is truly sovereign in salvation and in election and reprobation, men will have no reasons to do good works. They will think they can sin, because if they are elect they will go to heaven even if they do sin. They can sin as they please. And if they are reprobate, they will be sad and despair because no matter how many good works they try to do, they will never get to heaven. That is what Rabanus said Gottschalk was teaching. That argument is always false. That is a lie.

Rabanus accused Gottschalk of teaching that "the predestination of God binds all men in such a way that even if someone would want to be saved and would struggle for this by...good works...he would labor in vain...if he has not been predestined to life."[2]

Rabanus also put it this way:

This sect has led many into despair over themselves so that they say: "Why is it necessary for me to work for my salvation and eternal life? For if I do good but I have not been predestined to life, it profits me nothing. But if I do evil, it is in no way an obstacle for me. For the predestination of God causes me to come to eternal life."[3]

These things were not true. Such statements cannot be found in Gottschalk's writings. Yes, Gottschalk was teaching a sure and unchanging eternal decree of God that includes election and reprobation, but that doctrine never leaves one reprobate in despair nor one elect careless to do good works. No reprobate truly wants to do good works in order to glorify God, and no elect wants to sin, not in his inmost being where the new man in Christ reigns within him. "For I delight in the law of God after the inward man" (Rom. 7:22), Paul confessed along with every elect child

Gottschalk preached and taught a sure and unchanging eternal decree
of God that includes election and reprobation.

of God. And that love and desire to do God's law means there is
a battle. "For the good that I would I do not: but the evil which
I would not, that I do...O wretched man that I am!" (vv. 19, 24).
But the victory is in Christ Jesus.

The Belgic Confession, the Heidelberg Catechism, and the
Canons of Dordt addressed these very accusations some seven
hundred years later.[4] But Gottschalk had to answer those charges
in his day.

The margrave's reaction to Rabanus' letter has been lost in
history. One of Gottschalk's archenemies wrote of the history later
and said that Gottschalk was shamefully thrown out of Frioul, but
that is not confirmed by other sources.[5] Gottschalk stayed under
the protection of Eberhard for a very long time. They knew each
other well.

It may be that the letter from Rabanus, coming from such a
highly respected archbishop and friend of the family, alarmed the
margrave and his wife and caused them, either sadly or angrily, to
tell Gottschalk that he must leave their midst and go away. It may

also be that Eberhard and his wife did not agree with what Rabanus had written in the letter because they were already well informed as to what Gottschalk taught, and they believed it. Eberhard, as a well-respected leader, would not be easily swayed. In addition, the letter was written in 846, and Gottschalk did not leave Frioul until 848. Did Eberhard ignore the letter so that Gottschalk could continue to preach? Or could Gottschalk be confronted with the letter only after he returned from Croatia? We do not know.[6]

There would be another meeting called in Mainz to deal with Gottschalk and his teaching about predestination. Gottschalk was informed about the letter from Rabanus and the upcoming synod. Gottschalk went to the synod not because he had been expelled from Frioul and was forced to go, but Gottschalk went willingly. Gottschalk went to defend the doctrines he loved and taught, defending them against what Rabanus had written. One historian says that Gottschalk went in offense rather than in defense.[7] He had been a popular preacher for ten years, and he knew he was preaching the truth. He thought he had nothing to fear.

CHAPTER 15

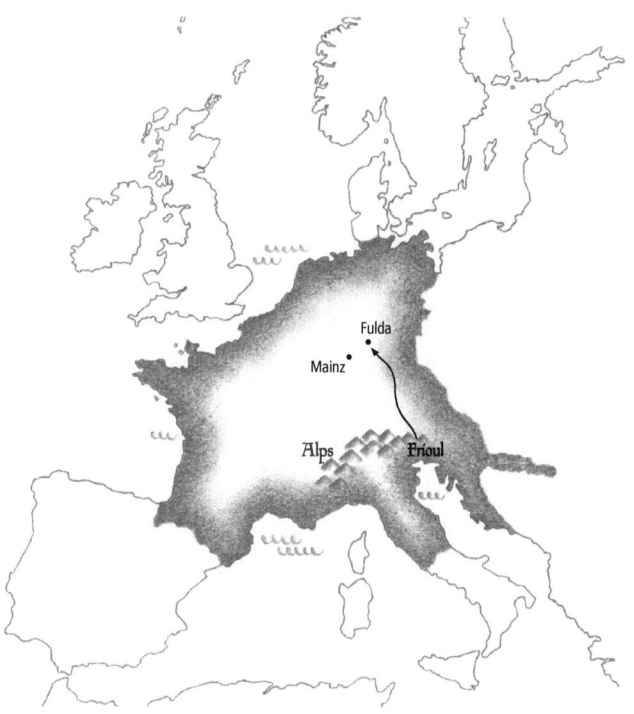

Gottschalk packed his satchel to travel north to Germany, his homeland, once more. Whether he climbed a pass through the Alps or plodded along some trail around them, he saw the awe-wrenching depths of the valleys and peaks of the mountain range along the way. It was a long trip. We can only imagine his thoughts as he journeyed.

A synod was scheduled for October 1, 848, in Mainz, and he had to be there to defend his doctrine. Gottschalk had attended two synods before, so the assembly he was heading to would not be an entirely new experience for him. While in his twenties he had been to Mainz for one of those synods and had seen the cathedral there.

Gottschalk, in his forties, would meet his old abbot, Rabanus Maurus, in Mainz. Rabanus had called for the synod against Gottschalk and his teaching. Rabanus was an archbishop then and in his seventies. He too was an older and more experienced man. He would be a formidable foe, able and fearsome in word and deed.

Gottschalk knew this man was not happy with him. Gottschalk saw all of Rabanus' letters and documents that he had sent to Bishop Noting and to Margrave Eberhard. Gottschalk saw what Rabanus had written about predestination over against Gottschalk's teaching about it. Rabanus' dislike for him was extreme. In Rabanus' mind Gottschalk was already a heretic. Gottschalk knew all those things, and he also knew he had to come to the Synod of Mainz prepared to answer all of Rabanus' accusations. A lot of thinking on the matter could be done while he trekked back north to the land of his Saxon ancestors.

It was either the end of summer or early autumn when Gottschalk arrived in Germany. A tinge of red and yellow adorned the trees. October 1 loomed in front of him, but he still had some time before that day would arrive. Gottschalk went to the monastery in Fulda, the place where his parents had brought him to live as a young boy so long ago. Other oblates were there to be educated and brought up as monks, as he had been. And Hatto, the new abbot, was there. Hatto did not share all of the same ideas with the former abbot, Rabanus Maurus. Hatto welcomed Gottschalk into the monastery.

Was it a pleasant experience, walking again among the same halls, seeing the same hills in the distance, hearing the same deep, melodious chants, the same majestic tower bells echoing in the sanctuary of the large church, and smelling the same kinds of dishes that were being prepared for Benedictine monks everywhere? It was all familiar to him, but did Gottschalk notice? He had other things on his mind and other things to do.

In Fulda Gottschalk made final preparations for the synod. He studied scripture and checked various writings and manuscripts of the church fathers, then he wrote down his own statements that he would present in Mainz. His arguments were logical, based on what Augustine had taught. More, they were based on what scripture teaches. Who can argue with scripture? Gottschalk was convinced that the doctrines of predestination and sovereign grace that he held to were good and right and according to the word of God. He had no doubt of it. Surely, he had nothing to fear.

In these final days before the synod, Gottschalk could be found working hard in the library and scriptorium in Fulda. Gottschalk knew his arguments would be important. The issues were immeasurably important. He knew his arguments needed to be clear and strong, and he counted it a privilege to be used of God to make them. He would be happy to stand before the synod and present those arguments there. The truth of God was at stake.

Gottschalk did not know that his life would be at stake too.

Gottschalk could be found working hard in the scriptorium in Fulda.

CHAPTER 16

abanus Maurus was at the Synod of Mainz in all the robes and vestments of an archbishop, and of an important archbishop at that. Louis the German, the king and ruler of the German part of the empire where Mainz was located, was there too. According to Rabanus' later report of the synod, "King Louis was presiding and in command" of the assembly.[1] The other bishops and abbots from that section of the empire were all there. Once more Gottschalk stood before kings and leaders of church and state. Once more he was asked to speak before important men of the world and to present his case.

The cathedral in Mainz.

This time, the issue was significantly—even infinitely—more serious. Rabanus brought the following charges against Gottschalk:

Gottschalk makes God the author of sin when he says that God decreed some men to be reprobate and to go to hell. Gottschalk's doctrine makes men careless and profane when he says that God brings all the elect to heaven no matter how much they sin. This is heresy.

Gottschalk defended his teaching before all those men. God gave him the strength and courage to do it.

Gottschalk quoted from scripture and from various church fathers concerning scripture, proving the doctrines he believed and taught. He stated his arguments "in the joyous conviction that it was in accordance with the doctrine of the church."[2] He was absolutely sure. He had to be. One does not stand before such mighty and important men in a church assembly if one is not sure that he is right before God and the church. He presented to the men, including the king, two pieces of writing that he had carefully prepared. One was an answer to Rabanus Maurus, and one was a very brief confession of his faith.

What we know of his answer to Rabanus Maurus is in bits and pieces because the whole document has not survived. We know some of what Gottschalk wrote from others who quoted it and whose quotes still exist. Gottschalk answered Rabanus, who had said, "The reprobate are not also divinely predestinated to damnation."[3] Rabanus did not like the decree of reprobation. He agreed that there was some kind of election, because that cannot be denied according to scripture. But Rabanus wanted works to be part of salvation too. He did not want to say that reprobation was decreed in the same way as election. Gottschalk said that reprobation was included in God's eternal decree of predestination just as election was.

Some of the things Gottschalk spoke of in his answer to Rabanus are as follows:

> Even as He has predestinated all the elect to life solely through the gracious favor of His grace, as the pages of the

Old and New testaments sharply and soberly testify with most clear evidence to us; so also He has certainly pre-destinated everyone who is reprobate to the punishment of eternal death, through the most just judgment of His unchangeable justice.[4]

All whom God wills to be saved, without doubt are saved: neither are any able to be saved, except those whom God wills to be saved: nor is there anyone whom God wishes to save and who is not saved, because our God has done whatsoever He has willed.[5]

Gottschalk said that if election is true, reprobation is true as well. They go together. To elect some is to reprobate others. Predestination is one decree with two parts. God chose some people to be his own dear children merely because he wanted to—not because of anything they did or would do. That means others were not chosen, also according to his sovereign will. Also, those who go to hell justly go there because they are indeed sinners.

Gottschalk quoted Augustine concerning the example of Judas Iscariot. God certainly determined Judas to be a reprobate and used him to bring about the circumstance of Jesus' death on the cross to save the elect. Nevertheless, God justly condemned Judas for doing that. Gottschalk quoted various texts from the Bible, including Jude 4: *"Certain ungodly persons crept in, who long ago were marked out for this judgment."*[6] Reprobation does not make God the author of sin. Rather, election together with reprobation makes God the author—the sole and only author—of salvation.

Even as Gottschalk saw the truth of election and reprobation as double predestination, God also opened Gottschalk's eyes to see other points of doctrine that must also be true if double pre-destination is true, such as the doctrines of particular grace and limited atonement. God shows his grace and love only to those whom he has elected, and Jesus died on the cross only for those elect. This is logical. This is scriptural. This shows that God is truly God. He does all his will, and he does not change his will.

God cannot change his mind about bringing one of his elect to heaven. If he wants to bring his elect to heaven, he will. Gottschalk saw this teaching in Psalm 135:6: "Our God *has done* all things *whatever he willed*."[7] The fact that God does not change spoke volumes to Gottschalk. A god who can change is not God.[8] An election that can change and be lost is no salvation at all.

Gottschalk was completely confident in presenting his arguments. They would be hard to refute. Of sovereign and particular grace he said,

> Therefore, what I believe most firmly, speak most confidently and confess most certainly and fruitfully, I also now most truly avow: that our omnipotent God, Creator and Preserver of all creatures, may be considered as the gracious renewer and restorer of the elect only; He has never willed at any time to be Savior of any of the reprobate; nor Redeemer; nor crowner.[9]

God elects whom he wills and reprobates whom he wills, and he does not change his mind about it. Christ died only for the elect, and no elect can ever be lost.

CHAPTER 17

One might wonder if Gottschalk was being proud and arrogant in daring to come to Mainz and to proclaim so bold a testimony there. How could he have the courage to speak so plainly and so contrary to Rabanus Maurus of Mainz, the most renowned and famous theologian of the day? How did he dare to confront the king to his face?

One might wonder also if Gottschalk was being simple and naive.[1] Did he not know that his arguments would be squashed by the long-established teachings of the church, teachings that for centuries were contrary to what Gottschalk said, teachings that supported the monastic way of life?

How could Gottschalk have the courage to speak before bishops and kings?

He was determined to be at Mainz. He had to give an answer. Does not scripture tell us to "be ready always to give an answer" (1 Pet. 3:15)?

We do not know what Gottschalk thought the outcome of the synod might be. He knew about the Synod of Orange (Or-ANHZH) held in 529. That assembly of bishops had decided that Augustine's teachings about sovereign and particular grace were partly true, but not completely true. And that synod had said almost nothing about predestination.[2] The decision taken at Orange was still the official position of the church at the time of Gottschalk.

At best, it can be said that the Roman Catholic Church in the early Middle Ages was not strong in the doctrines of grace; at worst, the church at that time did not hold to sovereign grace at all, at least not in practice. The mass and the monastic system showed that, and those things were not going to change. Since the time of Augustine, even though some statements in favor of sovereign grace had been made at Orange, they were by no means a solid defense of that truth. The church had not become stronger in its doctrines of grace, but weaker. There seemed to be even more confusion about those doctrines.

None of this mattered to Gottschalk. He was not confused about those doctrines. He was ready to make the truth of them clear. Only the truth of the word of God mattered to him.

Gottschalk's confidence was in the word of God alone. In the conviction of holding to the truth of scripture, Gottschalk was able to stand before all those men in the cathedral of Mainz, all alone, with such courage. Yes, other men in the Roman Catholic Church agreed with Gottschalk's teachings about predestination and particular grace. Many people did, in fact. A few friends even accompanied him to the synod. But that did not change the circumstance that Gottschalk stood all alone there to defend the doctrine of double predestination before those great men of the world and church. The charge of heresy was against Gottschalk alone.

73

We read of a similar situation in Psalm 119:45–47: "And I will walk at liberty: for I seek thy precepts. I will speak of thy testimonies also before kings, and will not be ashamed. And I will delight myself in thy commandments, which I have loved."

There is an explanation for this confident confession. The explanation was written down many centuries later, but the explanation holds true for all time. It explains the psalmist's stand for the truth. It explains Gottschalk's stand for the truth. It explains the reformers' courage as they held to the doctrines of grace in the face of all the persecution heaped on them during the sixteenth century. It will explain the strength of Reformed Christians who must stand for the truth in the last days of earthly history before Christ returns on the clouds of glory. The explanation is this:

> This certainty of perseverance, however, is so far from exciting in believers a spirit of pride, or of rendering them carnally secure, that, on the contrary, it is the real source of humility, filial reverence, true piety, patience in every tribulation, fervent prayers, constancy in suffering and in confessing the truth, and of solid rejoicing in God.[3]

What gave Gottschalk such confidence? The very truth he was confessing. That truth is "the real source" of all piety, prayers, and strength to confess the truth.

What was that truth? Election—sovereign, unconditional election. Reprobation—because only if God has sovereignly and justly ordained some men to reprobation does sovereign and unconditional election stand. And particular grace—God loves only the elect and purposes to save only the elect for whom Jesus Christ died. In these truths only is salvation sure.

Gottschalk was sure of that salvation. Gottschalk was sure of *his* salvation. That is "certainty of perseverance." It was a certainty that God would carry him without fail to eternal glory. In that knowledge, in that assurance, and in that faith Gottschalk had boldness to speak before great men and kings. Assurance is a gift worked by the Holy Spirit in all God's people. The Holy Spirit was working such assurance and certainty in Gottschalk then.

Gottschalk had prepared the following confession of faith, which he spoke before the Synod of Mainz:

> I, Gottschalk, believe and confess, profess and testify, from God the Father, through God the Son, and in God the Holy Spirit, and affirm and assert before God and His holiness that predestination is double whether of election to peace or of reprobation to death. Because just as God, by free grace, has unchangeably predestinated all His elect to life eternal, so likewise (*similiter*) the same unchangeable God by a just judgment has unchangeably predestinated all the reprobate, who in the day of judgment are damned on account of their evil merits, to merited eternal death.[4]

CHAPTER 18

Rabanus Maurus told the men at the Synod of Mainz that what Gottschalk said was heresy. King Louis the German agreed. So did the rest of the bishops and abbots sitting there. Gottschalk was a heretic. That was their final verdict. It is likely that King Louis, as head of the synod, pronounced the words of their judgment. The sound echoed within the high, hollow-domed ceiling of the cathedral-turned-courtroom in Mainz. The sound resonated higher still as saints under the altar in heaven cried, "How long, O Lord, holy and true?" If this day in October of 848 in Germany was not cold and stormy in weather outside, it was that in heart inside the grand building that was supposed to be used for the glory of God.

"But bold, hard, proud and disobedient characters he [the abbot] should curb at the very beginning of their ill-doing by stripes and other bodily punishments."

—St. Benedict's Rule, "What Kind of Man the Abbot Ought to Be"

Gottschalk's hands were bound. He was led outside into the streets of Mainz. His back was bared. He was whipped in sight of all those who passed by. His companions were treated the same. In addition, Gottschalk was forced to swear an oath that he would never again set foot in the realm of Louis the German. He was exiled from his homeland forever.

The sentence was severe. This had never happened before.

The Roman Catholic Church of that

day, according to *St. Benedict's Rule*, allowed for a monk to be severely beaten, including being flogged or whipped.

There had been unruly monks before. But something happened at the Synod of Mainz that was different. The church had never before condemned and punished a man because he was holding to the truths of double predestination and sovereign grace.

The church claimed to respect their church father Augustine with great admiration and honor. Augustine, who had lived from 354 to 430, had taught the doctrines of sovereign grace and predestination over against a man named Pelagius. Pelagius wanted to say that man is born good and he is able to live without sin. He does not need God's help and grace to be saved. But Augustine said there is no good in man at all; God must do all the work of salvation. Man cannot even help in his salvation.

"In this matter therefore we grieve that ecclesiastical truth has been condemned, not a wretched monk."[1]

During Augustine's lifetime the church agreed with Augustine in that teaching, at least in part. The church agreed that God is all-powerful to save, and that means the decree of predestination, including both election and reprobation, is true. How so? Because that decree explains the difference between those who are saved and those who are not. It is up to God's decision and power, not man's. Gottschalk pointed out these things regarding Augustine's teachings, things that Gottschalk was teaching then. In condemning Gottschalk, the church was rejecting the doctrines that Augustine taught, the same doctrines that Reformed believers embrace today.

This was a rejection of the truth of the word of God. Though the church had been doing this bit by bit for centuries through its various practices, by officially calling Gottschalk a heretic the church was in a much deeper way denying the scriptures. This was a denial of the scriptural doctrines of election and reprobation that Gottschalk stood for. That was serious. In Orange in 529, about a hundred years after Augustine, the church had failed to use and apply the truth of predestination. In Mainz in 848 the church openly condemned it.

And more, the church persecuted one who held to these doctrines. That was serious as well. That was new. The church had crossed a line when she did that.[2] The Belgic Confession states that the false church "persecutes those who live holily according to the Word of God, and rebuke her for her errors."[3] Gottschalk, by making his firm confession of election and reprobation, had rebuked the church for her errors. Either Gottschalk was right concerning election and reprobation or the church was right. If Gottschalk was right, the church was wrong. That was a rebuke. Gottschalk was persecuted for stating the truth.

October 1, 848, was a sad day in church history. It was a significantly sad day for all time.

CHAPTER 19

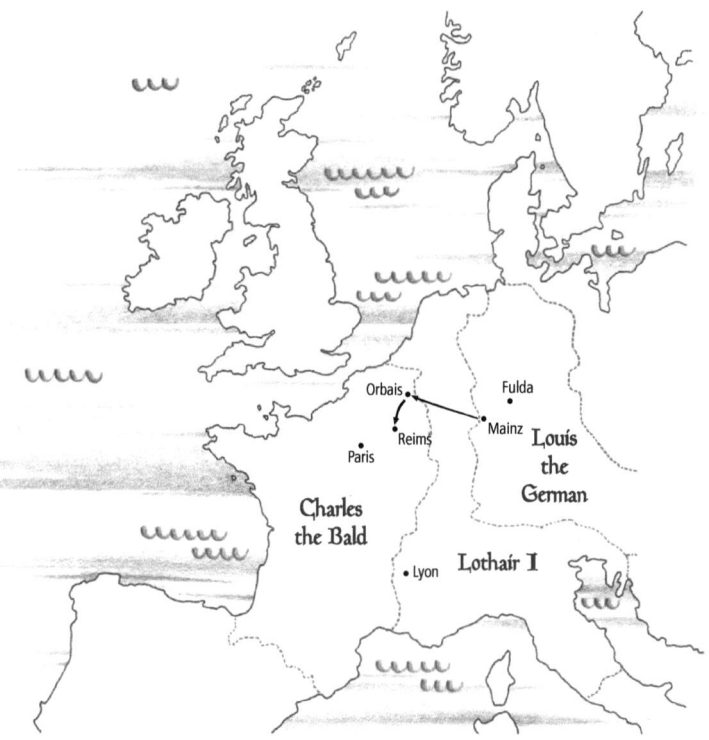

Orbais
Fulda
Mainz
Reims
Paris
Louis
the
German
Charles
the Bald
Lyon
Lothair I

abanus, the archbishop of Mainz, had his way with Gottschalk. The missionary monk was condemned and punished as a heretic. Now, what to do with him? Gottschalk could not stay in Mainz or in Fulda. Both towns were in the territory of Louis the German, and Gottschalk was banished from that section of the empire. Besides, Gottschalk had friends in Fulda. Hatto, the current abbot there, supported Gottschalk. Rabanus certainly would not want him living in a monastery where he had friends.

Legally Gottschalk should go to the monastery of Orbais in France where he had taken his final vows to be a monk. France was in the realm of Charles the Bald, the stepbrother of Louis the German. Gottschalk was not banished from Charles' territory. Gottschalk had friends in Orbais as well. Some of the monks in that monastery were well acquainted with the thinking of Gottschalk. Rabanus likely would not want him staying there either, at least not for long. So where could he stay? Who would consider him to be a heretic and treat him as such?

Hincmar, the archbishop of Reims, was Rabanus' man. Rabanus may not have personally known Hincmar, but he knew something about him. Hincmar had been a good friend of Emperor Louis the Pious before he died, even as Rabanus had been Louis' friend. That meant they very likely had similar opinions about things. Hincmar might see Gottschalk as a heretic even as Rabanus saw him as one. Besides, Reims was in France and the monastery of Orbais was in France in the same district over which Hincmar had charge, so there was a legal connection too.

Rabanus wrote a letter to Hincmar about Gottschalk. He sent the letter to Hincmar along with the condemned monk. According to one translator, part of the letter read as follows:

> We send to you this vagabond monk, in order that you may shut him up in his convent, and prevent him from propagating his false, heretical, and scandalous doctrine.[1]

Another translator records parts of the letter in this manner:

> Let it be known to your charity that a certain wandering monk, by the name of Gottschalk, who asserts that he is a priest ordained in your diocese, came from Italy to us at Mainz, introducing new superstitions and a harmful doctrine about God's predestination and leading people into error...

Therefore, hearing from him this opinion at a synod recently held at Mainz where our most pious King Louis was presiding and in command and finding him incorrigible, we decreed to send him condemned with his pernicious doctrine back to you.[2]

In the letter Rabanus continued to accuse Gottschalk's doctrine in the same way he had written about it to Bishop Noting and Margrave Eberhard, saying that people who listen to this doctrine will no longer care if they do good works or not.

For, as I have heard, he already has led astray and made them less devout toward their own salvation, who say, "How will it profit me to labor in the service of God? For, if I have been predestined to death, I will never escape it. But if I live badly and I have been predestined to life, I will without any doubt go to eternal rest."[3]

Rabanus concluded the letter to Hincmar, "You will also be able to hear more fully from his own mouth what he thinks and then justly decide what should be done about it."[4]

The message to Hincmar was that Gottschalk was a vagabond monk, a useless wanderer. He was stubborn and incorrigible and could not be convinced of his error. And worst of all, Gottschalk's doctrine was causing people to sin. Hincmar must hear and judge the monk and his poisonous doctrine, and then he must do something about it.

CHAPTER 20

The days were getting colder. October was well into the colors of the season. Every breeze took more leaves off the trees. The mood in Mainz was no less chilled. Gottschalk, still nursing the effects of the flogging on his back, must travel once again. Every jolt of every step could still be felt in the wounds. Guards of the diocese of Mainz were assigned the task of escorting Gottschalk to Orbais and then to Reims, where Hincmar the archbishop was stationed. The guards kept close

Guards were assigned to escort Gottschalk to Orbais and then to Reims.

watch over their prisoner. It was a lonely march of about 260 miles to Orbais and another 35 miles to Reims through wooded hills, valleys, farms, fields, and towns.

Steeples of churches and spires of cathedrals could be seen in the distance as they approached the cities and villages. Towers and bulwarks of fortresses and castles could be glimpsed on some of the most strategic hills. Gottschalk saw the golden and rusty colors of autumn, heard the crunch of fallen leaves beneath his feet, and smelled the dying vegetation and misty cool air that marked the changing of another season. Would the sights, sounds, and smells of autumn cheer him? Perhaps. God does all his will in the realm of nature as well as in the lives of men. For one who knows God's electing love, the truth of God's providence in creation is a comforting doctrine. As a poet, Gottschalk was sensitive to such beauties. Otherwise, for Gottschalk little was warm or pleasant about this long, cold journey from Mainz to France.

Castles could be glimpsed on some of the most strategic hills as they traveled.

Having reached Orbais, Gottschalk had a short time to again study the doctrines he was defending. He knew the library of that monastery well. He had studied the manuscripts there before, looking into the writings of Augustine, the works of Fulgentius of Ruspe and Isidore of Seville, and other church fathers from times past. They were all men who had seen the doctrine of election and reprobation on the pages of scripture even as Gottschalk saw it then.

Rothad of Soissons (Swa-SONH) was a bishop whose position put him in charge of the area in which Orbais was located, and even he understood and liked what Gottschalk taught. No, Gottschalk was not alone in his thinking and doctrine. At that moment in history he would have to continue to defend the doctrine alone. He would have to face Archbishop Hincmar alone. But he was not alone. If the colors of autumn had not cheered him, surely the pages of scripture, the writings of the church fathers, and some of his old friends at Orbais would.

But this small pause to study and renew acquaintances would not last long. Hincmar was wondering what to do with the Benedictine monk, and Hincmar was ready and waiting for him. It was time for Gottschalk to move on. Autumn was changing into winter. The leaves on the trees were gone. The walk would be even colder, and rain was more likely in that season. Gottschalk felt the icy, damp air in his nostrils as he and his guards set out together on the rutted, muddy roads of the early Middle Ages.

Finally the grand towers of the majestic cathedral in Reims, one of the most important cities of northern France, came into view.

An early-nineteenth-century painting of the cathedral in Reims.

84

CHAPTER 21

Archbishop Hincmar had read the letter from Rabanus Maurus, archbishop of Mainz, regarding Gottschalk. The archbishop saw the miserable monk standing before him, guards flanking either side of the cowl-hooded man. Hincmar and Gottschalk were about the same age—in their forties. Both were well educated. The similarities between the two ended there.

Hincmar took seriously the letter from his fellow archbishop. He questioned Gottschalk about his teachings. Gottschalk answered honestly and truthfully. The scars on his back, barely healed, did not change his views. Gottschalk had time to think about these things as he marched on the cold road to Reims. When once again called upon to answer for his teachings, he could try to prove more fully and carefully what he believed from scripture and the church fathers. But no, he would not change his views. By the grace of God, he would not.

Hincmar saw that he had trouble on his hands. The man standing before him was indeed stubborn. He did indeed teach double predestination, as Rabanus had warned him. And the monk was not afraid to say what he believed, even after being flogged. That was not a good sign—not for Hincmar. The challenge was on. He set out to break the man named Gottschalk, born of former pagan Saxons in Germany.

From Hincmar's viewpoint, Gottschalk was a dangerous man. He spoke too freely and too boldly, and he had too many followers. Hincmar also knew that Gottschalk had a history in Reims. Many

85

Hincmar saw that he had trouble on his hands.

years ago he had spent some time there, while making his way to join the monastery in Orbais. Gottschalk also had been friends with Ebbo, the archbishop in Reims at that time. A serious rivalry existed between Hincmar and Ebbo. That Gottschalk had been a friend of Ebbo did not endear him to Hincmar at all.[1]

Furthermore, while Gottschalk had lived with Ebbo in Reims years ago, he had traveled around teaching his views about predestination. People had heard him and believed what he taught. Too many people still remembered him and believed what he said. Yes, to Hincmar, Gottschalk was a dangerous man. Gottschalk must be dealt with, and dealt with quickly and severely.

Rabanus had instructed Hincmar to judge Gottschalk for himself. Gottschalk had been condemned in Germany, but as a legal resident of France, he also must be judged in France.

Charles the Bald, the king of Hincmar's section of the empire, planned on holding a synod soon with all the bishops in his territory to decide matters that concerned "the king's affairs."[2] In the Middle Ages kings helped rule in the business of the church, and the church helped rule in the business of the state. As an archbishop in Charles' territory, Hincmar could add items to the agenda of the meeting of synod if he wanted to. He was a powerful man. He added Gottschalk's case. He hoped that would quickly and easily mark the end of the whole matter.

Rabanus had guessed rightly. Hincmar viewed Gottschalk as a heretic and would treat him as such. But did the archbishop of Mainz guess the extent to which the archbishop of Reims would go to pursue further the destruction of the vagabond monk? That we do not know.

CHAPTER 22

Quierzy
Reims
hautvillers

incmar kept Gottschalk confined in Reims. The wandering monk would do no more wandering while he was under Hincmar's watch! Winter was well begun. Gottschalk waited. The cold rains that accompanied the season's dark days made the time pass slowly. He waited for the synod called by Charles the Bald to be held in late winter or in the early spring of 849, perhaps in March. The exact date is unknown. At this synod Hincmar planned to present Gottschalk's case to fourteen bishops and to the king. Hincmar waited for the synod too; he wanted to proclaim Gottschalk a heretic and to be done with him.

Fifteen bishops, one king, one monk, and a number of spectators
gathered in the royal villa of Quierzy.

The day came soon enough. Fifteen bishops, one king, one monk, and a number of spectators gathered in the royal villa of Quierzy (Keer-ZEE), about 55 miles northwest of Reims. The building was a large, grand manor fit for a king. The room in which they met was tall and spacious, decorated in ornaments customary for royalty. Guards and servants stood in attendance. The king and members of the synod were seated to consider the current business of the empire. Charles the Bald called the session to begin.

Charles was a young king, not quite twenty-six years old at that time. He was interested in the case of Gottschalk set before that gathering by the archbishop. Hincmar was an advisor and a strong supporter of Charles. That was important in those days of political connections and confusion between church and state. But Charles was interested in matters of religion for religion's sake as well. He showed that later when he asked men in the church to clarify and better explain to him the doctrine of predestination. Besides that, Walafrid Strabo, Gottschalk's old friend, had been Charles's tutor when the prince was a child. Charles perhaps did not know about the friendship between his old teacher and the accused heretic standing before him, or even that Gottschalk had for some time stayed in the castle of Charles' older sister Gisela and her husband, Eberhard. But Charles knew Hincmar was his own good friend then. Charles would listen to what the older, wiser archbishop had to say about Gottschalk's doctrines.

Hincmar included Gottschalk's priesthood in the discussion. Hincmar claimed that Gottschalk had been made a priest illegally while he lived in Orbais many years ago. A bishop was supposed to ordain men into the priesthood. But the bishop of the diocese where Orbais was located did not ordain Gottschalk—the bishop under that bishop did. Hincmar used that in his arguments against the monk.

Hincmar made his case. Just as at the Synod of Mainz, Hincmar presented Gottschalk as a heretic before all the men assembled at Quierzy. And just as at Mainz, Gottschalk was prepared to read and state his views to defend his doctrine, proving from scripture and from the church fathers that what he taught about double predestination and particular grace was true. He even had more proofs along with him, including more writings of Augustine and other trusted church fathers. He spoke at Quierzy with no less conviction and no less courage. He believed what he said with all his heart. The song of Psalm 119:45–46 rang true once more.

> And I will walk at liberty
> Because Thy truth I seek;
> Thy truth before the kings of earth
> With boldness I will speak.[1]

Gottschalk explained how God is not unjust when he elects some men and reprobates others. "What if God, willing to shew his wrath, and to make his power known, endured with much longsuffering the vessels of wrath fitted to destruction" (Rom. 9:22)? God does what he wills, and he is holy and righteous in everything he does. God is unchangeable. "With whom is no variableness, neither shadow of turning" (James 1:17). That means his decree, including election and reprobation, is forever sure. We do not know the exact words of Gottschalk's argument, but we know that his prepared refutation consisted primarily of proofs from scripture and from the church fathers.[2] Gottschalk used Romans 9:22 and James 1:17 in some of his later writings.

The synod heard Gottschalk's proofs and voted. Three of the bishops sided with Gottschalk. Twelve did not. Gottschalk's own abbot from Orbais and Bishop Rothad of Soissons said nothing in his defense. The result? Gottschalk was declared a heretic. We can only guess how the words struck the heart and soul of the accused monk and preacher who stood alone in the royal courtroom of Quierzy. Some witnesses said that Gottschalk spoke harshly at this point, but if he did, there is no record of those words either.

Heresy was a serious crime. Heresy is sin against God and his truth, a sin that divides the church and scatters the sheep. Of this awful crime Gottschalk was once again found guilty—Gottschalk, who had loved the truth from his youth and would love the truth to his death. Yes, the words hit him sorely, perhaps more than the leather of the whip that had only five months ago lashed his flesh.

Gottschalk had prepared in writing what he would say at this synod. So had Hincmar. Hincmar had the sentence ready to pronounce upon the guilty monk standing before the assembly:

> The ecclesiastical sentence pronounced with ecclesiastical force by twelve bishops at the synod held at Quierzy against the most stubborn Gottschalk because of his incorrigible obstinacy:
>
> Brother Gottschalk, know that the sacrosanct [priestly] office of the sacerdotal mystery [sacrament of the mass], which you irregularly usurped and have thus far not feared to abuse in all evil morals and actions and perverse teachings has been taken from you...In addition, because, for

showing contempt of ecclesiastical laws, you have presumed to disturb both ecclesiastical and civil affairs contrary to the life and name of a monk, we decree by episcopal [bishop's] authority that you be punished with the severest beatings and that according to ecclesiastical regulations you be confined to a cell, and lest you presume to usurp [unlawfully take] for yourself the teaching office, we impose perpetual silence on your mouth by the power of the eternal Word.[3]

The stubborn and rebellious Gottschalk was no longer allowed to be a priest. The office was taken from him. He was to be beaten severely. He must stay in a prison cell of a monastery. And he was ordered to silence so he could no longer teach his doctrine. The result was worse than at Mainz.

Gottschalk was led outside the villa, still holding the parchments he had written. A fire was built. The wood crackled as the heat from the blaze grew. Gottschalk was ordered to throw his writings and doctrinal proofs into the fire. He stood still. He did not. For a few moments the only movement was rising smoke. Many witnesses looked on.

The last of his painstakingly written pages were consumed in the flames.

The order was made for Gottschalk to be flogged until he threw his writings into the fire. Gottschalk still did not. Not right away. One historian wrote, "According to the report of eye-witnesses, he was scourged 'most atrociously' and 'nearly to death,' until half dead he threw his book, which contained the proofs of his doctrine from the Scriptures and the fathers, into the fire."[4] His blood stained the ground. The last of his painstakingly written pages were consumed in the flames.

Perhaps the outcome of this synod was not a complete surprise for Gottschalk. He had suffered before, being scourged for teaching the truth of scripture. That time had been a great surprise, but it showed him what could happen. In the face of that knowledge he still did not recant.

If anyone was surprised at Quierzy, it would have been Hinc-mar the archbishop of Reims. He knew from Rabanus Maurus what Gottschalk had experienced at Mainz. Why would that man be willing to suffer such things again? Was something wrong with the man? It likely made no sense to Hincmar. If anything, it made him despise the monk all the more. Perhaps it made him fear the monk all the more. The tremendous courage of Gottschalk in all those events was undeniable. Hincmar did not like what he saw. Hincmar had won his case against the man, but that had not changed the man at all.

Bleeding, bruised, and wounded, Gottschalk was escorted from the grounds of the villa to the monastery in Hautvillers, about 15 miles south of Reims. A prison room was in that abbey. That was where Gottschalk would stay.

CHAPTER 23

And I will walk at liberty? Because thy truth I seek? Gottschalk was locked in some type of room, prison cell, or dungeon in Hautvillers. He had no freedom or liberty—no physical liberty. But freedom is more than physical. Prisons are more than stone walls and iron bars. The liberty Gottschalk had was spiritual. Gottschalk had sure knowledge that all his sins were gone—banished from the sight of God forever. *That* is freedom.

Along with that, Gottschalk was free from the guilt of having denied the truth of scripture, from having denied his Lord who saved him. Jesus is the truth, Gottschalk knew. Gottschalk had

Gottschalk was locked up in Hautvillers.

confessed the truth before ruling churchmen and kings to the best of his ability by the grace of God. He had suffered two floggings within five months' time. He had been repeatedly reproached and slandered because of his doctrine. He was held in a prison. Anything could happen in medieval prisons. But God had given him grace to stand firm, to hold to the truth through it all. That is freedom and liberty indeed.

A view of the monastery in Hautvillers as it appears today.

Gottschalk was in good company. Jesus had warned that such reproach and persecution would come. The apostle Paul had experienced those same kinds of things—Paul, who had clearly and specifically taught the truths concerning God's sovereign, particular grace and twofold predestination in his letter to the Romans. Paul wrote of his experiences: "Five times received I forty stripes save one. Thrice was I beaten with rods, once I was stoned, thrice I suffered shipwreck" (2 Cor. 11:24–25). No, Gottschalk dare not compare himself to that apostle to the Gentiles who received instruction in true doctrine directly from the risen and ascended Lord, but the example of Paul's life and teaching was there.

The example of Christ was there: "For what glory is it, if, when ye be buffeted for your faults, ye shall take it patiently? but if, when ye do well, and suffer for it, ye take it patiently, this is acceptable with God. For even hereunto were ye called: because Christ also suffered for us, leaving us an example, that ye should follow his steps" (1 Pet. 2:20–21). Gottschalk was walking in those steps. He was suffering for doing well. He would never come out of this dungeon again.

He would never again see the blazing autumn forests of Germany, the golden harvest fields in France, the snowcapped peaks of the Alps, nor any other grand and glorious sights in God's creation. But Gottschalk had seen those things, and he had seen much more. He had seen the glorious and beautiful truths of his God. There is nothing grander than that. And Gottschalk would see more of that beauty. God was not yet finished with assigning labors to his servant. Paul wrote letters from prison. So would Gottschalk—not inspired letters like Paul's were, but Gottschalk had work to do.

The deep wounds on Gottschalk's back began to heal. Remarkably, he was also allowed to continue to write in Hautvillers. How this came about we do not know, for he had been ordered to silence at Quierzy. That meant no writing. Did the abbot or other monks in Hautvillers ever get that message? Did they secretly agree with Gottschalk and keep him supplied with parchments and ink? Was he allowed to use the library there? Perhaps he quoted so many texts from his excellent memory. Perhaps his guards saw no harm in letting Gottschalk use his time in this way. Did friends come to visit him and smuggle in what he needed and smuggle his letters out? Or perhaps Hincmar did not enforce that part of Gottschalk's sentence, because Hincmar feared an outcry from Gottschalk's followers and friends. However it happened, Gottschalk made good use of the opportunity.

He had been forced to burn the parchments that contained the proofs for what he taught, proofs from scripture and the church fathers. He wrote these things down again, this time in the form of two confessions—one called a *Shorter Confession*, aimed especially at defending the doctrine of reprobation, and one called a *Longer Confession*, treating double predestination and other related topics. He wanted to explain clearly his teachings, and these writings still exist today. He wrote in Latin, but what he wrote has been translated into English.[1] In the providence of God these documents have been preserved and are evidence of

God's faithfulness to continue to reveal the truth of his sovereign particular grace in all ages.

Gottschalk alone held the honor of being so persecuted in that hour of history for holding to the true doctrines of election and grace, but the issues that Gottschalk's trials and imprisonment brought to the foreground were far from over. His story was not finished yet. Hincmar was not done with the whole business, as he had hoped.

CHAPTER 24

Gottschalk heard the thud of the prison door and the clink of the key in the lock. The sound would accompany the simple meal brought to him every day. His food likely consisted of a trencher-type piece of flat bread with some vegetable stew on top. No plate or utensils were provided except for a cup or ladle for something to drink. The monks, freely eating together in the refectory, required little more for themselves, although they might have enjoyed a few extra dishes to choose from that the man locked in his cell did not see as he ate and drank alone. Food was not guaranteed, however. According to *St. Benedict's Rule*, forced fasting was sometimes used as a form of punishment in monasteries.

In the Middle Ages dungeons were often built into the basements of large structures. This could have been the case for Gottschalk's place of imprisonment. Perhaps an iron-barred window let in some light—and chilled air. Some comforts were allowed. Gottschalk was given wood to build a fire to combat the cool draft. Perhaps a cot or table was there for him to rest on, but we do not know. Furniture was precious and scarce in the Middle Ages. Even in a well-to-do home the same kitchen table was used for dining, working, writing, and for servants to sleep on at night. Whatever other possessions Gottschalk had behind the locked door, we know he had some ink and a quill.

Hincmar wrote, "In the lodge where he lives he has a fireplace and a toilet."[1]

Perhaps an iron-barred window let in some light.

As soon as Gottschalk recovered enough from the punishment heaped upon him at Quierzy, he began to write many letters. He even wrote to Hincmar, and Hincmar wrote back to him! They first wrote each other concerning the issue of predestination, but how to speak properly of the Trinity became an issue between Hincmar and Gottschalk as well. No words were spared in either man's writings. They strongly and vehemently disagreed on both subjects.

Hincmar tried to get other theologians to pick up his cause against Gottschalk concerning the Trinity, but almost no one did. We are not sure why. Perhaps Hincmar's and Gottschalk's arguments seemed too detailed to be of concern. Whatever the reason, that issue was not pursued by others. The subject of predestination was another matter, however. That issue became a boiling pot of heated debate among provinces, bishops, and kings throughout the whole empire. Hincmar might have wished this subject had never been brought up at all!

How was it that the issue of predestination become so earnest and so widespread throughout the whole church of western Europe? Through letters.

It was in response to Hincmar that Gottschalk wrote his *Longer Confession*, a document written in the form of a deeply felt prayer to God that laid out Gottschalk's explanations and proofs for the doctrine of double predestination. But Gottschalk also wrote about predestination to many other leading theologians in the empire. Many of them agreed with his doctrine, either in whole or in part. Ratramnus of Corbie and Abbot Lupus of Ferrières (Fair-ee-AIR) were two with whom Gottschalk exchanged letters, and they supported his views. Some theologians in southern France especially liked what Gottschalk taught, such as Deacon Florus of Lyon (Lee-ONH) and Remigius.

Besides all this, news of the terrible things that had happened to Gottschalk was spreading. Some theologians expressed their concerns over Gottschalk's treatment. They were alarmed. What had the church done to a fellow preacher? Even if he was only a monk or priest in rank, the seriousness of the deed was clear to all even then, not just from the perspective of later history.

Hincmar seemed to have second thoughts—not about his own doctrinal stand, but about what ought to be done with Gottschalk. Other theologians were writing about predestination. What happened to Gottschalk made people think. Gottschalk's letters to important theologians made those important men think. And some of them were leaning in Gottschalk's direction. Hincmar became alarmed.

In addition, for other reasons Hincmar was already not popular with everyone in the Roman Catholic Church. Just as royal princes can fight and war with one another for more lands and power, when authority in the state and authority in the church becomes mixed up, men can also fight for offices of power in the church. Some men coveted Hincmar's lofty position as archbishop of Reims. Ebbo was still trying to get the position of archbishop back for himself. Other clergymen and even King Lothair, a step-brother of Charles the Bald, were also against Hincmar. He had enemies in the kingdom. The issue about predestination was not helping him.

Hincmar wrote a letter addressed "to the monks and simple folk" of the area surrounding Reims.[2] He was worried that those who had heard Gottschalk preach a number of years ago believed his doctrine, and his doctrine continued to spread. Hincmar had good reason to worry. When the sheep hear the voice of their Shepherd, they follow. In the truth of sovereign, unconditional election the sheep were hearing that voice. Hincmar did not want that to happen. In the letter he tried to make Gottschalk sound like he "was the devil himself."[3]

On all sides of the issue parchments were flying in every direction.

CHAPTER 25

The reproach of the condemned monk, even after he was cast into prison, did not stop. In Hincmar's public letter, written in the autumn of 849 to the "monks and simple folk" of his diocese, the archbishop of Reims wrote that Gottschalk was "long known to us by the rotten reputation of his wretched way of life and by the abomination of his perverse preaching."[1] Hincmar continued,

> I have heard...he poured the worst venoms into your hearing and also into your hearts...teaching that there are some predestined to punishment which no one predestined can escape, no matter what good or how much good the person does, and no one predestined to glory, no matter what evil he does, can perish...He...introduces a pernicious security...He also teaches that the death of Christ was not celebrated for the salvation of the whole world.[2]

Hincmar went on to describe a letter by Gottschalk, written to a monk named Gislemar in Corbie. Gottschalk had found friends at the monastery in Corbie before he took his monastic vows in Orbais. Gislemar was one of those friends. Somehow Hincmar received a copy of Gottschalk's letter to Gislemar, and Hincmar seriously criticized it by writing that Gottschalk "speaks great blasphemies instead of praise."[3]

Blasphemies? That is a strong word. That was the same false charge pressed upon Jesus at his trial before Caiaphas the high priest. That is what the antichrist will speak in the very last days. What blasphemies did Hincmar accuse Gottschalk of writing? The following statement was taken directly from Gottschalk's letter to Gislemar:

> God forbid that I should ever want to dream or only to whisper that the ancient serpent might be able to carry off with him into eternal perdition any of those for whose redemption such precious blood of our Lord his Son has been poured out to God the Father. Amen.[4]

Anyone familiar with the five points of Calvinism will recognize two of those points in these words of Gottschalk. Limited atonement: Christ died only for the elect. Preservation of the saints: not one elect is lost. God forbid, said Gottschalk, that I even whisper that Satan might ever be able to steal one of Christ's sheep away with him into hell.

Blasphemies instead of praise? "The reproaches of them that reproached thee fell on me" (Rom. 15:3, quoting Ps. 69:9). There is no greater praise to God than to confess that God is almighty to do all his good will and that his will cannot be thwarted. Not one of his beloved sheep can be snatched out of his fatherly hand. There is no greater comfort than knowing this doctrine is true. This is blasphemy? No, the Reformed man will love and defend this "inestimable treasure" to the end.[5]

CHAPTER 26

The dampness of the cold winter rains seeped into the stone walls of the monastery in Hautvillers. Gottschalk, wounded with many stripes, had been brought there in early spring after his trial at Quierzy. Summer came and went, and winter came again. All was alike to Gottschalk, locked away within the stony depths of the abbey—all alike except for the cold.

According to Hincmar, Gottschalk was given wood to make a fire, clothes to stay warm, food to be sustained, and water to take a bath, which water Gottschalk reportedly refused.[1] If all this is true, we do not know why Gottschalk refused the wash water. Maybe he was trying to live somewhat like the hermits of that era. Hincmar also said that his prisoner was insane and that the devil possessed Gottschalk's mind.[2] That was cruel reproach.

That Gottschalk's mind was somehow affected by all the tribulation pressed upon him at the monastery was possible. One historian says Gottschalk's prison cell became a "torture chamber."

Another historian says that Gottschalk's "rather mild conditions...in Hautvillers" were not so bad as to cause mental illness.[4] Another historian is not so sure that Gottschalk had a mental disorder

"The cruel Hincmar... was determined to force Gotteschalk to recant. Within the walls of the monastery Gotteschalk was whipped so severely that he nearly died. But as he lay on the floor of his torture chamber, bloody and near death, he continued to refuse to retract his position."[3]

at all, because as he wrote, "Hincmar had a vested interest in persuading his readers that Gottschalk was mentally deranged!"[5] Whatever the case may have been, another church historian wrote, "[Gottschalk] had the courage of his convictions. His ruling idea of the unchangeableness of God reflected itself in his inflexible conduct. His enemies charged him with vanity, obstinacy, and strange delusions."[6]

Although his enemies also charged him with demon possession, there was no demon in that man's heart and soul. Without doubt the Holy Spirit dwelled in that servant of God. No man can understand any doctrine in truth without the Spirit's revealing it to him. We know Gottschalk understood doctrine in truth. His ability as a theologian was great. His confession never wavered. His logic never failed. No demons dwell where the Spirit of Christ lives.

Although we are unable to judge what may or may not have been some illness of mind in Gottschalk, it is well to note that when one confesses the truth of scripture, those who reject that truth often hurl accusations of madness and demon possession at that person. Jesus said that his servants would be treated even as he was. And so it is. As Gottschalk was a servant of Jesus Christ, we can expect the same accusations to be thrown at the monk as were thrown at his Lord. Jesus endured the same cutting words from many, who said, "He hath a devil, and is mad; why hear ye him?" (John 10:20).

But others said, "These are not the words of him that hath a devil. Can a devil open the eyes of the blind?" (v. 21). As Gottschalk went about preaching the truths of sovereign grace and double predestination, God used that preaching to open the eyes of many people—to open their spiritual eyes to understand more of God's truth. That is what true preaching does. If anything, all that proves what a servant of God Gottschalk really was.

Hincmar claimed his prisoner was treated reasonably well by those who watched over him. But Hincmar also had called

Gottschalk a stubborn heretic and had called his doctrine pernicious, venomous, blasphemous, and more. Those are all strong
words. Hincmar had seen Gottschalk's blood dripping once
before. And Hincmar still greatly desired Gottschalk to recant,
to say that election and reprobation as God's own appointment
was not true, and to say that Christ died for all men. That could
require more punishment, more threats, and more persecution.

This may indeed be what happened, causing a mental
breakdown in the severely ill-treated man.[7] Others say Hincmar
continued to try to get him to recant but began to use softer
means.[8] The historian Neander wrote that Hincmar "hoped to win
the man to submit by gentleness, whose will could not be broken
by force. But at the demand of Rabanus Maurus, Hinkmar soon
resorted again to new severities against the unfortunate monk."[9] It
is safe to say that if Hincmar did use harsh means, he might have
tried to cover that up. He was already under criticism for having
Gottschalk treated so cruelly at Quierzy.

Some things in Gottschalk's life might seem odd to us who
live so many centuries after the early Middle Ages. But those
things were not strange for that time in history. In Gottschalk's
Longer Confession he offered to submit to a "trial by ordeal." Such
a trial was a longstanding custom in the Frankish kingdom,
involving the endurance of some kind of torture as a last resort to
prove one's innocence.

Gottschalk said he was willing to step into four heated barrels,
"individually filled with boiling water, oil, pitch, and animal fat,"
and if he should come out unhurt, that would prove he was not
a heretic at all.[10] However, neither Hincmar nor anyone else
challenged Gottschalk to attempt this awful trial, so he did not go
through with it. We might wonder if some of his opponents were
just a little worried that Gottschalk might miraculously survive
that ordeal, but it is more likely that they considered the ordeal to
be untrustworthy and unfair, proving nothing except the hurt of

the person involved. Later in the Middle Ages the trial by ordeal would no longer be accepted practice in the church. But it was still a practice during Gottschalk's time, although some theologians frowned upon the idea.

In doctrine, Gottschalk was a man out of time. His thoughts were remarkably close to those of the reformers of the sixteenth century. The same doctrines Gottschalk was beginning to develop would not be developed again until some seven hundred years later by Martin Luther and John Calvin. That Gottschalk would not evidence any miracle by using the trial by ordeal is not surprising. That he did evidence a miracle of grace and faith in his confession of the doctrines of double predestination and limited atonement—confessing them alone in the ninth century against much opposition—can be claimed. Gottschalk was indeed a man out of time.

What actually happened in that prison cell in northern France? Gottschalk continued to write theologically and to write well, at least as long as he was allowed to do so. One historian says that freedom only lasted about a year.[11] Gottschalk was never set free. He spent the rest of his life behind a locked door within the monastery.

Hincmar showed no mercy at Quierzy in having Gottschalk severely flogged and punished at that time. Hincmar continued to try to get Gottschalk to recant, using whatever means he chose. Hincmar never let Gottschalk partake of the sacrament of bread and wine again. He thought about letting him. He asked others for advice. But he never did. In that regard there was no softening on the part of Gottschalk's accuser.

Gottschalk suffered as a prisoner. By that time he was well into his forties. But while he was enduring such affliction being locked away from the world, many things were happening outside his cold and stony prison walls.

CHAPTER 27

Hincmar had a bishop under him, an assistant named Pardulus. Hincmar told Pardulus to write to some of the most respected theologians in the church about predestination. Hincmar wanted to know what they thought about the issue. One man named Prudentius, the bishop of Troyes (Trwah), wrote back. Hincmar especially valued the opinions of Prudentius. But Prudentius' letter sounded very much like he agreed with Gottschalk's doctrine. Could that be true? Hincmar also heard about a sermon preached by a theologian named Florus of Lyon—a sermon that was critical of Hincmar's views. Hincmar was hearing other things as well. He was becoming worried.

Hincmar, from Reims in France, wrote to his fellow archbishop in Germany, Rabanus Maurus of Mainz, who had sent Gottschalk to Hincmar in the first place. Hincmar sent to Rabanus the letter written by Prudentius of Troyes along with a number of other letters. The packet included copies of Hincmar's own letters, Gottschalk's letters, and other churchmen's communications, both for and against Gottschalk. Hincmar wanted to know what Rabanus thought about it all. Rabanus was older and more experienced in such things, and Rabanus and Hincmar thought alike concerning Gottschalk and his doctrine. Surely Rabanus would help.

Rabanus wrote back several months later that Prudentius of Troyes indeed agreed with Gottschalk. But that is all the elderly Rabanus said. Hincmar must deal with Gottschalk and his doctrine alone. Hincmar had also asked Rabanus about allowing

Gottschalk to partake of the sacrament of the bread and wine. Although Rabanus did not want to be involved in the case anymore, he did answer the question. He said no. Gottschalk was a heretic, and he ought not to have any bread and wine to assure him of the forgiveness of his sins.

In the meantime, Emperor Charles the Bald—Hincmar's own ruler over France—began asking questions. What really is the truth about predestination? What is the truth about free will and sovereign grace? The emperor, who had seen everything that had happened to Gottschalk at Quierzy and had even been a part of it, was asking friends of Gottschalk for the answers. Ratramnus, a very strong supporter of Gottschalk, sent his answer to the king about those things. Yes, Hincmar was getting very worried.

Pardulus wrote a letter to John Scot Erigena, a famously educated theologian from Scotland who came to France to live in the palace of Charles the Bald. Only a handful of men in western Europe knew Greek at that time, and Erigena was one of those few. That made him special. But if Hincmar and Pardulus hoped that man could straighten everything out, their hopes were soon dashed. Yes, Erigena strongly opposed Gottschalk. But Erigena also made claims and statements about predestination and other religious matters that were clearly heretical to all, whether one was for Gottschalk's doctrine or against it. Everyone became upset. Hincmar was in even more trouble.

Predestination was becoming too big of an issue to be dealt with by writing letters back and forth. Respected churchmen were on both sides. Even Emperor Charles the Bald wanted answers. With all those opinions about predestination swirling around the empire of western Europe, who was right? The church must decide. More synods were needed to settle the issue. But whether or not this would help Gottschalk remained to be seen.

CHAPTER 28

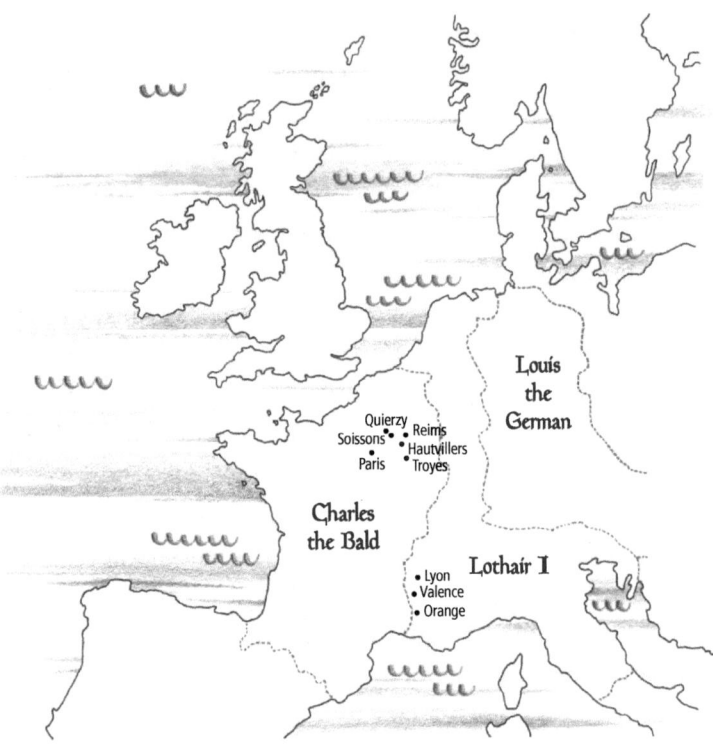

Iow could one monk in one prison cell cause so much controversy in the whole Roman Catholic Church of the European Frankish kingdom? In the providence of God he could. But the monk did not cause the controversy. When the word of God is distinctly and clearly set forth, it divides the truth from the lie. It also divides those teaching and believing the truth from those teaching and believing the lie.

Small points of doctrine tossed about in letters will not cause much trouble. But the doctrines of election and reprobation are no small points to argue. Believing the truth about the decree of election and reprobation affects everything. Gottschalk wrote, "Truly, O Lord, if it is better that none of Thy elect had been created (or saved) than that Thou shouldest be changeable (or changing), how much more then is it impossible that thou shouldest be changed on account of the vessels of wrath and anger."[1] God was using Gottschalk to be a witness to that truth. He was indeed God's servant in that labor. Hincmar had a deep and real controversy on his hands.

Hincmar had other problems too. His position in the church had always been in danger. Ebbo, the former archbishop of Reims, and other important men in the church had been against Hincmar from the beginning. About that time in the predestination controversy, a case concerning Hincmar's office of archbishop came up for a vote at a council in Soissons, France. Was Hincmar the real archbishop of Reims or not? That was the question. It was a serious question. Not long ago Hincmar had forced the office of priesthood to be taken away from Gottschalk; now Hincmar's office was in doubt. If Hincmar were no longer the archbishop, that could greatly affect what would happen in the predestination controversy and with Gottschalk.

What was the result of Soissons? Hincmar won his case. Hincmar's place as archbishop of Reims was finally safe. He could turn all his attention to the issue of predestination. In God's full control of history, Hincmar did. God controls all things for the good of his elect children, even if it does not always seem so.

Hincmar called for another council to decide how the church ought to understand predestination. Too many people were siding with Gottschalk. Hincmar, having been confirmed in the office of archbishop, had the power to try to stop that.

The council was held in Quierzy in 853. The men of the synod, each seated in their special place of title and honor in the royal villa, heard Hincmar speak his views. Hincmar said that man is free to choose to do good or evil; he has a free will and is able to choose the good. God chooses his elect by looking ahead to see what good works they will do. Christ died for all men on the cross because he wanted all men to be saved. Because all these things are true, said Hincmar, reprobation in eternity does not exist. God does not choose men to go to hell; he only chooses men to go to heaven.

We can imagine many of those important men, dressed in the fine robes of their various offices, nodding in agreement as Hincmar spoke. Likely, he spoke what many of them had always believed. Everything Hincmar said went together with the whole system of monks and monasteries and nuns and convents that had been ingrained in the life of the Roman Catholic Church. Hincmar said nothing new.

Gottschalk was not present to hear the arguments, but the idea of what Hincmar was saying was clear: Gottschalk's teachings were wrong. As happened once before, the sound of the church's decision about these doctrines bounced off the lavishly decorated walls of the royal villa of Quierzy and landed with the same woeful thud. Yes, Gottschalk was wrong. There is no double predestination. Christ died for all men. Gottschalk was not there to point out that if all this were true, God is a god who can change his mind depending on what man does. He is not God anymore.

Gottschalk may have been locked away in prison, but Charles the Bald was present. Despite having received a letter from Gottschalk's friend Ratramnus explaining the truth of double predestination, the king approved of all of Hincmar's conclusions.

Other people in the empire did not. Men in the church of Lyon in the southern part of the empire picked up their quills and started writing against what the council in the northern part of the empire had done. The church in Lyon agreed with Gottschalk's views, and Lyon was in the realm of King Lothair, the royal brother who ruled the part of the empire between Charles' realm and that of Louis the German. A battle of words went on for months. Just as Charles the Bald had been concerned about understanding those doctrines, so was Lothair.

Lothair, the older brother of Charles, called for a council to be held in January of 855 in Valence (Va-LAHNHS), a city in Lothair's territory. The council in Valence made decisions against the council in Quierzy that had been held a few years before. King Lothair was not physically well. One of the last things he did before he died that same year was to make sure the decisions of the Valence council were written down and delivered to his younger stepbrother, Charles the Bald. The brothers did not agree. The issue of predestination was still far from being decided. Kings were divided over it too.

Still more synods would have to be held. It appeared nothing was going to be settled without compromise, even though compromise means no victory for the truth. Would that happen? Men wanted the issue to be finished.

Four years later, in 859, a group of bishops from the south gathered together to rewrite the decisions made in Valence so that they would not be so sharp and offensive to Hincmar and his supporters in the north.

Soon after in that same year, another council was held in France to deal with the compromise that the southern bishops had written. This time all three kings of the Frankish kingdom were there: Charles the Bald, Louis the German, and Lothair's son. Surely with all those kings present and with so many other bishops and important clergymen there—and with compromise on the table—the issue would be settled. But it was not. That synod was promptly postponed for political reasons. In the providence of God a compromise that would have destroyed the truth was delayed.

CHAPTER 29

Finally, one more synod was held to decide the church's position concerning predestination. That one would end the matter. The gathering met in a royal villa in Touchy (Too-SHEE), France, in October of 860, exactly twelve years after Gottschalk had first been tried and condemned as a heretic in Mainz. Like a pot of boiling water, the church had been in a growing turmoil over the doctrine for twelve years. In Touchy over forty bishops from fourteen provinces throughout the whole of the Frankish kingdom gathered to hear and to decide about the truth of predestination.

All the men at the synod must have known about Gottschalk, how he had suffered being whipped and was still locked in his monastery prison cell because he dared to be a witness to what he believed. If those men did not know that, they most assuredly knew that Augustine, who so strenuously fought against the teachings of Pelagius in the fifth century, was a church father to be studied and revered. Each man stood, one by one, to state his loyalty to the teachings of Augustine, the man whom Gottschalk had so often quoted and understood so well. We can imagine

Each man stood, one by one, to state his loyalty to the teachings of Augustine.

their hands, raised in solemn oaths, as each one repeated something of this sort: "I believe and promise to uphold all that our faithful father Augustine has so truthfully taught."

We can only wonder what Gottschalk would have thought had he been there to see that show of loyalty to his dear father in the faith. Would the church finally fully embrace what Augustine truly taught? Would the Roman Catholic Church see the truth of double predestination and the lie of Pelagianism in all its forms after all? Gottschalk had merely seen and brought to light what Augustine so long ago had taught about those things. The church back then agreed that Augustine was right, although in life and in practice the church also showed that it disagreed with him.

It was the ninth century. Would the church finally agree fully with Augustine? That was the issue. To agree with Gottschalk was to agree with Augustine. With their loyalty to Augustine so clearly spoken to one another at the Synod of Touchy, they showed that they understood the issue. How could they decide any differently than to support what Gottschalk was teaching?

But he who struts about the world as a roaring lion, seeking to devour whomever he may, also dresses as an angel of light. He knows how to work the lie. He is the father of it. He can make his roaring purr like a kitten.

The arguments about election and reprobation proceeded. The men at Touchy listened carefully. Hincmar presented the doctrine of predestination in language that was not distinct or clear. What he said could be understood to agree with either Hincmar's view of election, which had no room for reprobation in the decree at all, or with Gottschalk's view, which included both election and reprobation in God's eternal decree.

Hincmar's proposal passed. But it was no solution, nor was it in reality any compromise. If the truth is not clear, the truth is lost. Hincmar won the church. The lie would hold full sway.

The boiling pot of water was turned down to a very low simmer.

CHAPTER 30

All seemed lost. Gottschalk continued to languish in his prison cell, losing strength and health day by day and year by year. The Roman Catholic Church—the only church of that time in western Europe—had decided against the truth of election and reprobation in God's decree of predestination. In rejecting this basic doctrine, that church would never be strong to grow in her understanding of doctrine and truth again. The church was languishing too. Israel's slavery in Egypt must have looked as bleak. What would become of it all?

These were the Dark Ages. But a light had shown forth. A witness had been made. The record of it was there, although the days would continue to grow spiritually darker still. He who rules in heaven rules the hearts of men and Pharaohs. He controls it all for the salvation of his people. He would raise up more servants of God, even as Gottschalk was, qualified by the Holy Spirit to see and to discern the truth of the word of God and to sound the warning. They too would speak of election and reprobation and of limited atonement and of grace, and they would clearly and loudly proclaim those doctrines far and wide.

But that would take a long time. Hundreds of years must pass. In the meantime, the Roman Catholic Church made it clear that such witness to the truth would not be tolerated. The only way to grow in the doctrines of grace would be to come out of the Roman Catholic Church and to join another one. God would work that all out in the great Reformation of the 1500s.

The time for that worldwide Reformation was not yet ripe.

The light of the truth, although by no means as bright as it would shine in the sixteenth century and not as bright as it was shining almost all alone then from one prison cell in Hautvillers, still flickered. It would continue to do so. The Spirit's witness in the hearts of his own can never be extinguished. That, indeed, was part of the doctrine Gottschalk was being persecuted for. In his *Longer Confession* he prayed, "Neither permit these things to be doubted by any of Thy elect (which is impossible)."[1]

Hincmar held the reins of the church in the realm of Charles the Bald in France, but there was another man living even farther south than Lyon, in the renowned city of Rome, a man who had more authority in the church than even the archbishop in France did. Pope Nicholas I became aware of Gottschalk's situation. In all of Gottschalk's letters to leading theologians of the Roman Catholic Church, Gottschalk had not forgotten this head clergyman. Gottschalk's letter to the pope had been smuggled out of Hautvillers by a monk named Guntbert. Monks were not allowed to leave their own monasteries without permission, so Guntbert was risking severe punishment to escape the abbey to do this. Nevertheless, somehow he was able to safely deliver the message. We do not know what consequences he may have had to endure for following through with the plan. Gottschalk still had faithful friends.

So where did the pope stand? A document recording church history from 859 states: "Nicholas, the Roman pontiff, faithfully confirms and in a catholic manner determines his position concerning grace and free will, as well as concerning the truth of the twofold predestination and the blood of Christ, which was shed for all believers."[2] According to this report, the pope said that double predestination was true! He agreed with Gottschalk.

This opinion of the pope in Rome was not used at the synod of 860 in Touchy, however. Either his thoughts were not known in France or they were ignored. Hincmar later wondered if that report was true. But in 863 Nicholas did make it known that he wanted Hincmar to appear together with Gottschalk before his representatives at a council in Metz. The pope wanted to hear more about Gottschalk's case. That meeting did not take place, however. Hincmar said he got the message too late, though some historians doubt the truth of that excuse.

Pope Nicholas died four years later in 867. Gottschalk died five years later, around 868. Was there time to call another meeting before they died? We do not know. So we cannot be sure how strong that stand of Pope Nicholas I was. The light was there, flickering. But it was not flickering much.

CHAPTER 31

God maintains his truth in the world despite the workings of men. Indeed, he uses them. All was not lost. This was God's plan. Everything that happened to Gottschalk and in the church was in God's immutable, eternal counsel and decree. That decree of his plan has everything to do with his unchangeable decree of election and reprobation, and the certainty of that decree was exactly the comfort that kept Gottschalk to the very end of his life.

Gottschalk was held captive in the depths of the monastery in Hautvillers for approximately twenty years. He died there. He was allowed to write for a time. But we do not know how many more times he was flogged in efforts to get him to recant. Hincmar never let him partake of holy bread and wine, nor did he allow Gottschalk to be buried in the grounds of the church. His name was not included on the list of all those dead monks whom a committee of living monks would pray for every day for years and years, according to their custom. But that did not matter. The Savior had prayed for Gottschalk that his faith fail not. It never did.

As Gottschalk breathed in his last gasps of musty prison air, Hincmar tempted him. The archbishop sent a three-point *schedula*, or set of written statements, to Hautvillers for Gottschalk to sign. If he signed the parchment, he could partake of the sacrament of bread and wine before he died, and he could be buried in the grounds of the church as a member of the church. If he refused, he could not.

What were the three points Hincmar wanted Gottschalk to agree to? Hincmar was subtle in his writing. First, regarding predestination, Gottschalk had only to agree that Jesus died for all men, that God gives salvation as a gift, and that some men refuse that gift. Second, regarding grace and free will, Hincmar merely said that Gottschalk had to agree with church fathers like Augustine and Prosper, although what that specifically meant Hincmar did not explain. Third, regarding the Trinity, Gottschalk had to agree with Hincmar's position, over against what Gottschalk had earlier argued concerning it. Just sign that sheet of parchment, Gottschalk, and you will not be considered a heretic anymore. You can be a member of the church again. You can have the bread and wine. You can have a Christian burial. You will not go to hell.

Gottschalk was physically ill. He was near death. Would he have the strength clearly to see these statements for what they really were? Being seriously sick and weary, it would be easy to give in. Hincmar was hoping for that.

Gottschalk was shown the *schedula*. Despite any former accusations of mental illness, he understood well the implications of what was written there. He refused to sign it. According to Hincmar's record of the event, Gottschalk became angry with the propositions set before him. He most certainly would not sign the archbishop's three points.[1]

But Hincmar did not give up. Gottschalk was not dead yet. Hincmar was not finished with him yet. He sent a list of instructions to the monks of Hautvillers, telling them to make every effort to get Gottschalk to recant. Hincmar impressed upon the monks how important that was. Gottschalk still might sign the *schedula*. He still might partake of the bread and wine before he died. The monks were to tell him that again and again. Thus this dying martyr was plagued to the last pulse and beat of his faithful heart.

Imprisoned, sick, and lonely, he feared denying the truth more than he feared anything else. In his *Longer Confession* he wrote, "For if it is possible I ought and should a thousand times die for

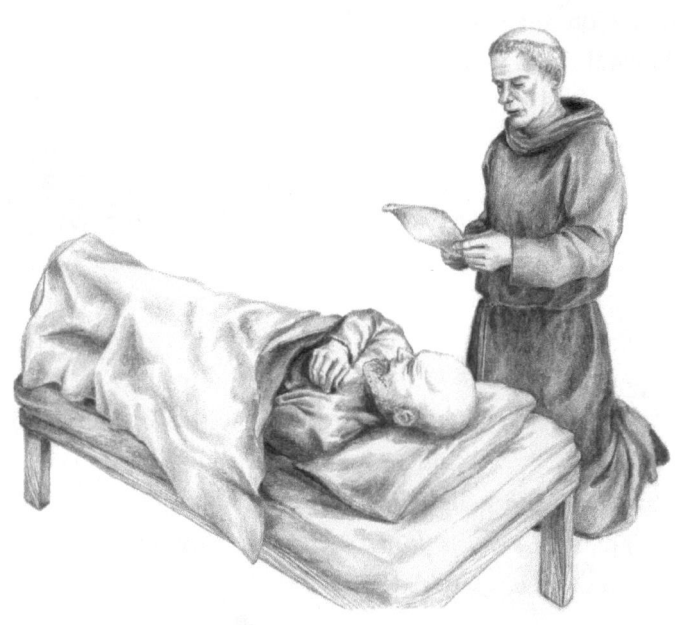

Hincmar told the monks of Hautvillers to make every effort to try to get Gottschalk to recant before he died.

the truth, than that once, by speaking against it, to give way and succumb; remembering that Thou knowest that: 'who confesses me before men, him also will I confess before My Father Who is in heaven' (Matt. 10:32)."[2] He never denied his Lord who had died for him.

There is no greater love than that a man lays down his life for his friends. And so it was. Gottschalk was safe in the arms of his Lord. Gottschalk laid down his life for his dearest Friend in heaven and on earth, his Friend having first laid down his life for him. And in that Friend's love Gottschalk was kept to the end.

Gottschalk knew that long ago in eternity God had chosen him to be an elect child of God in Jesus Christ for no other reason than that God wanted to. By himself Gottschalk was only a man, a sinner like everyone else. He knew that. The reason for election is in God alone. Gottschalk knew that too. God does not change his decrees. Gottschalk knew the devil cannot steal one elect out of God's hand. Even locked away in his prison cell, Gottschalk knew the devil could not steal *him*. His election and salvation was sure. His path in this life was sure. His place in heaven was sure.

In that knowledge Gottschalk could die for the truth he loved. In that blessed knowledge he did one autumn day, the thirtieth of October.[3] The servant is not greater than his lord and master. Gottschalk died, a witness to the truth, a true servant of him who is grace and truth to all ages and forevermore.

"All that Thou hast willed, Thou hast at the same time done."[4]

"Ye are my witnesses, saith the LORD, and my servant whom I have chosen: that ye may know and believe me, and understand that I am he...and beside me there is no saviour...therefore ye are my witnesses, saith the LORD, that I am God" (Isa. 43:10–12).

Appendix 1

GOTTSCHALK'S WRITINGS

Serious accusations were brought against Gottschalk in his lifetime. Did he ever answer them? He did. Perhaps not in specific words that state, "In answer to those charges," but he did answer. The Reformed faith has always drawn such charges. The Canons of Dordt say of these same accusations that they are those "which the Reformed churches not only do not acknowledge, but even detest with their whole soul."[1] For Gottschalk, his whole life and confession shone "more brightly than the sun" in answer to the same foul charges.

If it were true that the doctrines he taught could cause men not even to try to live a life of faith and good works, the main person lacking in faith and good works would have been Gottschalk himself. He really believed the doctrines of predestination and sovereign grace. But that did not leave him to sin as he pleased. On the contrary, his sins were to him "much weightier than a mass of earth." He expressed such grief in many verses of poetry.[2] Nor was Gottschalk careless to do good works. His godliness is abundantly evident in all his writings.

The words of this monk drip with humility and a deep desire to glorify God. His love for the truth cannot be denied. His faithfulness to the doctrines he found in scripture is clear—"clearer than light" itself. To one extent or another, other men at that time in history confessed these doctrines too, but only Gottschalk was required to seal his confession of these truths with his own blood. The gift of faith given to him was great indeed.

Some samples of Gottschalk's poetry and his *Shorter Confession* follow. His *Longer Confession* and *Extant Fragments* can be read at www.rfpa.org.

Gottschalk speaks for himself in this prayer:

Therefore, O God, by Thee being graciously emboldened through faith, made firm in hope, and likewise enflamed by love, I humbly implore that while giving to me true humility, Thou wouldest make me always to joy with real joy. Finally, to Thee and to Thy name be due glory forever...Amen.[3]

The following poem by Gottschalk has been loosely rewritten here in an attempt to include some measure of rhyme in the English.

A Hymn to God the Life-Giver

Freely in Thy goodness Thou hast created me.
Freely now, I pray Thee, create my life anew!
Freely are Thy gifts bestowed, free-flowing grace undue.
O Holy Spirit, Thou dost bring to instant life all who
By Thee are breathed into;
Together with the Father and His beloved Son,
Thou dost thunder forth in might,
Governing and giving light;
Thou dost increase and infuse
The faith which Thou dost grant
To whomever Thou dost choose.
Still more, Thou cleansest lepers
Polluted in their shame,
Ungodly men are righteous,
Made clean in Thy pure name;
Together with the Father and His beloved Son,
Thou recreatest souls,
All those of Thine elect,
And when Thy work is done,
Thy glory lights each one.[4]

Two more samples of Gottschalk's poetry have been translated by Jason Holstege, Jonathan Langerak, Jr., and Justin Smidstra. That Gottschalk is remembered in history along with the greatest poets of the medieval age is not without reason. It is well that his poetry, written to the glory of God, be remembered still today.

O Reverend Offspring of God

1.
O reverend Offspring of God,
Likeness of the Father glorious,
Unfathomed radiance, blessed light,
Thou floodest every land with light,
Yet Thou art ever with the Father.

2.
What Thou hast is nothing less than the Father,
A scepter Thou holdest with equal right;
Whatever Thou desirest, Thou art mighty to do;
For Thou dost renew and revive men,
Yea, for them Thou dost foster a fairer homeland.

3.
Thou makest the wretched safe and sound;
Thou biddest each one to forsake his sins.
Thou dost grieve that we have gone astray,
Warn us to return to our true homeland,
And teach us, O God, to repair unto Thee.

4.

I beseech Thee, answer now the humble prayers,
Which prayers, O King, I pour forth unto Thee.
And also, I pray, in my misery console me.
Yea, with Thy devotion enliven me
And from my sins far remove me.

5.

I pray: Strengthen me with all good things;
Let sin's plague no more oppress me,
But may I be found worthy to be Thy friend,
That I may have beloved rest,
Thy rest, which our elders did before attain.

6.

To them, O Christ, Thou showest Thy face,
Thy golden face shines forth;
Henceforth they are forever joyful
And gladly worship Thee in love.
I pray: O God, join me to them forevermore!

Nonae

1 The ninth hour! Thou didst mightily emit the spirit
2 And gave to us the prize of endless life,
3 And paid the price weighed by provident scales,
4 Piercing through our death's deep abyss
5 Light to darkness came, daylight flooding shadows,
6 When to Thine elect Thou didst allot snow-white robes,
7 But to the reprobate fiery judgment long deserved.
8 Hence we who fear and hope on Thee do ever pray
9 That thou drive the terror of eternal death far from us,
10 And take away from us the gloom of deepest night;
11 Guide them to the sweetness of life with Thee.
12 Thou art clothed in vesture white, with flashing presence,
13 Thou art pleasing and lovely, meek yet dreadful,
14 Thou art fair and beloved, the heart's desire,
15 Thou alone art immortal and without change,
16 Thou art holy and to be adored as both King and Lord.
17 Cleanse us, exceedingly foul and defiled with sins,
18 Illumine our minds, cause Thy light to fill our bodies,
19 That finally putting off the body, Thou might see us as white as snow.
20 Here I submit "Let it be" and "Amen," joining music with prayers.
21 Glory be to God the Father, to the Son, yea, to the Spirit,
22 To God triune yet one, in peace, in life, in light,
23 In name indisputably sweet, and in divine will.

ottschalk's *Shorter Confession* deals primarily with proving from scripture and the church fathers that the doctrine of reprobation is true. If election is really true, then reprobation is really true too. It was this doctrine—reprobation—that was especially disliked and denied by Rabanus Maurus and Hincmar of Reims, so it is not surprising that Gottschalk, writing from his prison cell in Hautvillers, aimed a whole confession in defense of this doctrine. Translated by Ronald Hanko.[5]

Confessio Brevior
Shorter Confession

I believe and confess that God, omnipotently and unchangeably, has graciously foreknown and predestined holy angels and elect men to eternal life, but that He in like manner (*pariter*) has, by His most just judgment, predestined the devil, who is head of all the demons, with all his apostate angels and also with reprobate men, who are his members, on account of their foreknown particular future evil deeds, to merited eternal death: this the Lord Himself affirms in His Gospel: "The prince of this world is already judged" (John 14:11). Augustine, beautifully explaining these words to the people (Augustine on John, tract. 95), has spoken as follows: "That is, he has been irrevocably destined to the judgment of eternal fire." Likewise concerning the reprobate, the same is true: "Who then believeth not is already judged" (John 3:18), that is (as the aforesaid author explains), (tract. xii), already is damned: "Not that judgment is now manifest, but that judgment is already wrought." Likewise explaining these words of John the Baptist: "His testimony no man has received" (John 3:32), he speaks in this wise (tract. xiv): "'No man,' is a certain people prepared to wrath by

God, damned with the Devil." Also concerning the Jews: "Those dead scorners, predestinated to eternal death." Again (tract. xlviii): "Why did the Lord say to the Jews: 'Ye believe not because ye are not of my sheep' (John 10:26), unless because he saw that they were predestinated to everlasting destruction, and not to life eternal by the price of his own blood." Also, explaining these words of the Lord (ibid.): "My sheep hear my voice and I know them and they follow me and I give to them eternal life, and they shall never perish, and no one shall snatch them out of my hand: my Father who gave them to me is greater than all, and no one is able to snatch them out of my Father's hand" (John 10:27–29), he says this: "What can the wolf do? What can the thief and robber do? They destroy none, except those predestined to destruction." Speaking in like manner concerning the two worlds (tract. lxxxvii) he says: "The whole world is the church, and the whole world hates the church; the world, therefore, hates the world, the hostile that which is reconciled, the damned that which is saved, the polluted that which is cleansed." Likewise (tract. cx): "There is a world concerning which the Apostle says: 'that we should be condemned with this world' (1 Cor. 11:32). For that world the Lord does not pray, for He certainly cannot ignore that for which it is predestinated." Likewise (tract. cvii): "Judas the betrayer of Christ is called the son of perdition as the one predestinated to be the betrayer." Likewise in *Enchiridion* (cap. 100): "To their damnation whom He has justly predestinated to punishment." Likewise in the book *On Man's Perfection in Righteousness* he says (cap. 13): "This good, which is required, there is not anyone who does it, not even one; but this refers to that class of men who have been predestinated to destruction: indeed, upon those the foreknowledge of God looks down and pronounces sentence." Likewise in the books *de Civitate Dei* (lib. xxii, c. 24): "Which is given to those who have been predestinated to death." Likewise blessed Gregory the Pope (Moral. lib. xxxiv, c. 2): "Leviathan with all his members has been cut off for eternal torment." Likewise holy Fulgentius in the third book *Concerning the Truth of Predestination and Grace* (lib. iii, c. 5) says: "God has prepared punishment for those sinners (at least) who have been justly predestinated to the suffering of punishment."

And blessed Fulgentius has composed one whole book for his friend Monimus concerning this tantamount question, that is: *Concerning the Predestination of the Reprobate to Destruction* (lib. i).

Whence also holy Isodore says (Sentent. II, cap. 6): "Predestination is double (*gemina*) whether of election to peace, or of reprobation to death." The same thing, therefore, (with others) I believe and confess, through whatever may happen, with those who are the elect of God and true Catholics, according as I am helped by divine inspiration, encouragement, and provision. Amen.

False, indeed, is the witness, who in speaking of any aspect of those things, corrupts them either superficially or with respect to their essential sense.

Appendix 2

TIMELINE

354	Augustine is born
430	Augustine dies
529	Synod of Orange
c. 540	*St. Benedict's Rule* is written
744	Boniface founds the monastery of Fulda
768	Charlemagne begins to reign
c. 780	Rabanus Maurus is born
799	Vikings make their first attack in the Frankish kingdom (on a monastery)
800	Pope Leo III crowns Charlemagne as emperor
c. 806	Gottschalk is born
806	Hincmar of Reims is born
814	Charlemagne dies; his son Louis the Pious begins to reign
822	Rabanus Maurus becomes abbot of Fulda
829	Synod of Mainz (concerning Gottschalk's claim about being a monk)
840	Louis the Pious dies

841	Battle of Fontenoy (between the sons of Louis the Pious)
843	Treaty of Verdun (assigning territory to the sons of Louis the Pious)
845	Paris is attacked by Vikings
846	Rome is attacked by Arabs
848	Synod of Mainz (Rabanus brings Gottschalk to trial as a heretic)
849	Synod of Quierzy (Hincmar brings Gottschalk to trial as a heretic)
853	Synod of Quierzy (Hincmar's statements concerning predestination are accepted)
855	Synod of Valence (some of Gottschalk's views concerning predestination are upheld)
856	Rabanus Maurus dies
859	Synod of Savonnières (compromise concerning predestination is attempted)
860	Synod of Touchy (final decision on predestination)
863	Pope Nicholas I orders Hincmar to a council in Metz (Hincmar fails to go)
c. 868	Gottschalk dies
882	Hincmar of Reims dies as he flees a Viking raid

ENDNOTES

PREFACE

1 Gottschalk, *On Predestination*, trans. Victor Genke, in Victor Genke and Francis X. Gumerlock, ed. and trans., *Gottschalk and a Medieval Predestination Controversy: Texts Translated from the Latin* (Milwaukee, WI: Marquette University Press, 2010), 121.

CHAPTER 1

1 Historians do not agree on the exact year of Gottschalk's birth because it cannot be determined with certainty, but it was likely between 803–6. Herman Hanko records it as 806. Herman Hanko, "Gotteschalk: Martyr for Predestination," in *Portraits of Faithful Saints* (Grandville, MI: Reformed Free Publishing Association, 1999), 68.

CHAPTER 2

1 This verse is from a poem written by Walafrid Strabo, translated in Peter Godman, *Poetry of the Carolingian Renaissance* (London: Duckworth, 1985), 227.

CHAPTER 3

1 The ceremony is recounted here as described in Editors of Time-Life Books, *What Life Was Like in the Age of Chivalry: Medieval Europe AD 800–1500* (Richmond, VA: Time Life Books, 1999), 19–20.

CHAPTER 4

1 St. Benedict of Nursia, "On the Clothes and Shoes of the Brethren," in *St. Benedict's Rule for Monasteries*, trans. Leonard J. Doyle (Collegeville, MN: The Liturgical Press, 1948), 77.

2 Ibid.

CHAPTER 5

1 St. Benedict, "What Kind of Man the Cellarer of the Monastery Should Be," in *St. Benedict's Rule for Monasteries*, 48.

Chapter 6

1 Richard C. Dales, *The Intellectual Life of Western Europe in the Middle Ages* (Washington, DC: University Press of America, 1980), 94–95. It is also interesting to note what this author says concerning the quality of this poem: "He devised one poem of such beauty and originality that it deserves quotation... And it stands two tests of great poetry; the beauty and pathos of the sound and rhythm are evident even to one who does not understand Latin; and the content retains its merit even in an uninspired prose translation." Ibid., 94.

2 Godman, *Poetry of the Carolingian Renaissance*, 231.

3 Philip Schaff, *History of the Christian Church*, (Charles Scribner's Sons, 1910; repr. Grand Rapids, MI: William B. Eerdmans Publishing Company), 4:525n.

Chapter 7

1 George H. Tavard, *Trina Deitas: The Controversy between Hincmar and Gottschalk* (Milwaukee, WI: Marquette University Press, 1996), 18.

Chapter 8

1 Kurtz, *Church History* (London: Hodder and Stoughton, 1891), 1:508.

2 Rabanus Maurus, *On the Oblation of Children*, trans. Victor Genke, in Genke and Gumerlock, *Gottschalk*, 17.

3 Ibid., 18.

4 Hincmar of Reims, *Letter to Pope Nicholas*, trans. Francis X. Gumerlock, in Francis X. Gumerlock, "Gottschalk of Orbais: A Medieval Predestinarian," http://www.kerux.com/kerux/doc/2203A4.asp.

Chapter 9

1 "If anyone should presume to say...that the wicked are foreknown but in no way predestinated; make that one, I pray, diligently to give heed to how he contradicts the truth...Show him (as holy Augustine says) that 'no changeable nature can be recompensed, unless Thou, O Lord our God, remainest unchanged.' Nothing is important if Thou, who art from eternity, art reckoned, yea, believed and preached by the church to be changeable in the day of judgment, and also in that same day of judgment, as it were, Thou shouldest be changed in that Thou dost not do what was predestinated, that is, sending the reprobate to torment. And so Thou shouldest be reckoned to be changed eternally, that is, to be mortal (which is impossible) for that which is changed also dies." Gottschalk, *Confessio Prolixior* [Longer Confession], trans. Ronald Hanko, in Ronald Hanko, "Gottschalk's Doctrine of Double Predestination," *Protestant Reformed Theological Journal* 12, no. 1, (November 1978):47.

CHAPTER 10

1 For the issues that Gottschalk talked about, see Hanko, "Gottschalk's Doctrine of Double Predestination," 32. "The issues in the controversy were really two. The central question was whether predestination was single or double, that is, whether it embraced some men or all men and their acts, whether good or bad. In connection with this was a second problem, the relation between predestination and foreknowledge."

2 Gottschalk, *Longer Confession*, trans. Ronald Hanko, in ibid., 44–45.

CHAPTER 11

1 Gottschalk, *Tome to Gislemar*, trans. Victor Genke, in Genke and Gumerlock, *Gottschalk*, 69.

2 Ibid., 70.

3 "Therefore I humbly entreat Thee, Thou Who are mightiest of all, most merciful and most glorious, Triune and one Lord God, that Thou wouldest graciously deign to be my equitable helper and hearer; and that Thou wouldest grant to me, who am most needy, through Thy unmerited grace, invincible courage in order that now I might truthfully and simply declare with my mouth unto salvation, that which out of Thee, in Thee, and through Thee I have long ago believed in my heart, and by Thy grace have confessed concerning Thy foreknowledge and predestination. Grant this, that through what I have done, truth invincible and blessed forever may at last be revealed to Thy elect and falsehood presently conquered and very justly condemned as it ought to be. Amen." Gottschalk, *Longer Confession*, in Hanko, "Gottschalk's Doctrine of Double Predestination," 44.

4 Gumerlock, "Gottschalk of Orbais: A Medieval Predestinarian."

5 In the course of writing about a battle he witnessed, Gottschalk wrote, "Gottschalk, my little son." Gottschalk, *Answers to Various Questions*, trans. Victor Genke, in Genke and Gumerlock, *Gottschalk*, 33. Some speculate this young man to be either his nephew or another such companion as dear.

CHAPTER 13

1 Rabanus Maurus, *Letter to Noting*, trans. Francis X. Gumerlock, in Genke and Gumerlock, *Gottschalk*, 28, 165.

CHAPTER 14

1 Rabanus Maurus, *Letter to Eberhard*, trans. Francis X. Gumerlock, in Genke and Gumerlock, *Gottschalk*, 166–67.

2 Ibid., 166.

3 Ibid.

4 Belgic Confession 24; Heidelberg Catechism Q&A 64; Canons of Dordt, 5.12; and others, in Philip Schaff, ed., *The Creeds of Christendom with a History and Critical Notes*, 6th ed., 3 vols. (New York: Harper and Row, 1931; repr., Grand Rapids, MI: Baker Books, 2007), 3:410–11, 328, 595.

5 It is possible that this enemy of Gottschalk added to and falsified some of the history as he replaced another historian who had already written about it. This is suggested by George Tavard: "[Hincmar] is likely to have added these lines to Prudence's text; Prudence did not share Hincmar's doctrine on predestination." Tavard, *Trina Deitas*, 52.

6 Victor Genke, introduction to Genke and Gumerlock, *Gottschalk*, 30–31.

7 "The confidence with which Gottschalk went to Mainz shows that he was altogether convinced that his ideas were orthodox, and he attacked rather than defended himself." Ibid., 30.

CHAPTER 16

1 Rabanus Maurus, *Letter to Hincmar on the Council of Mainz*, trans. Francis X. Gumerlock, in Genke and Gumerlock, *Gottschalk*, 167.

2 Hanko, "Gotteschalk's Doctrine of Double Predestination," 32, quoting Kurtz.

3 Gottschalk, *Reply to Rabanus Maurus*, trans. Francis X. Gumerlock, in Genke and Gumerlock, *Gottschalk*, 65.

4 Gottschalk, *Extant Fragments*, "Of Double Predestination," in Hanko, "Gotteschalk's Doctrine of Double Predestination," 62. This and all subsequent translations from *Extant Fragments* are by Ronald Hanko.

5 Gottschalk, *Extant Fragments*, "Concerning Free Will," in ibid.

6 Gottschalk, *Reply to Rabanus Maurus*, trans. Francis X. Gumerlock, in Genke and Gumerlock, *Gottschalk*, 66.

7 Ibid.

8 Gottschalk wrote that if God can change his mind in the day of judgment about who is elect and who is reprobate, then (speaking to God), "Thou shouldest be reckoned to be changed eternally, that is, to be mortal (which is impossible) for that which is changed also dies." He would no longer be God. Gottschalk, *Longer Confession*, trans. Ronald Hanko, in Hanko, "Gotteschalk's Doctrine of Double Predestination," 47.

9 Gottschalk, *Extant Fragments*, in ibid., 63.

CHAPTER 17

1 Genke, introduction to Genke and Gumerlock, *Gottschalk*, 37. "Gottschalk, a bit naive, was convinced that when he had shown to the synod that his

teachings were pure Augustinianism and in keeping with the Scriptures besides, he would be completely exonerated [declared innocent]." Herman Hanko, *Contending for the Faith: The Rise of Heresy and the Development of the Truth* (Jenison, MI: Reformed Free Publishing Association, 2010), 97.

2   "The synod's failure to call attention to the doctrine of predestination constitutes a serious omission on its part, an effort to compromise with the truth. And we may never compromise with the truth. Any compromise with the truth is always a surrender to the forces of the lie." Herman Veldman, "The Doctrine of Sin, The Third Period—730–1517 AD, Gottschalk," *Standard Bearer* 45, no. 5 (December 1, 1968).

Veldman also had this to say about the Synod of Orange: "Compromises never satisfy. And...Semi-Pelagianism is really more dangerous than outright Pelagianism. Any attempt which takes off the sharp edges constitutes a sinister attack upon the fundamentals of the Word of God." Herman Veldman, "The Doctrine of Sin, the Second Period—250–730 AD, The Pelagian Controversy, Semi-Pelagianism," *Standard Bearer* 45, no. 1 (October 1, 1968).

Pelagius was the opponent of Augustine. He said that man is basically good and can save himself by doing his own good works. Man does not even need the grace of God to do it. Semi-Pelagianism says that man is basically bad, but not completely bad. Man needs the grace of God therefore, but only for some help. Man can partly save himself.

3   Canons of Dordt 5.12, in Schaff, *Creeds of Christendom*, 3:595.

4   Gottschalk, *Extant Fragments*, in Hanko, "Gotteschalk's Doctrine of Double Predestination," 63.

CHAPTER 18

1   Remigius (in the name of the church of Lyon), "A Reply to the Three Letters," in George E. McCracken ed., *Early Medieval Theology,* Library of Christian Classics (Louisville, KY: Westminster John Know Press, 2006), 9:167.

2   In a letter written in the name of the church in Lyon, Remigius "condemned the unjust and cruel treatment of Gottschalk...Their mode of conducting themselves towards Gottschalk, he said, was regarded with universal abhorrence; for before this, all heretics had been refuted and convicted by words and reasons. In condemning Gottschalk's doctrine of predestination, men condemned not that unhappy monk, but the very truth *of the church* itself." Augustus Neander, *General History of the Christian Religion and Church*, trans. Joseph Torrey (Edinburgh: T & T Clark, 1850), 6:293-94.

3   Belgic Confession 29, in Schaff, *Creeds of Christendom*, 3:421.

CHAPTER 19

1 Hanko, *Portraits of Faithful Saints*, 70.
2 Rabanus, *Letter to Hincmar on the Council of Mainz*, trans. Francis X. Gumerlock, in Genke and Gumerlock, *Gottschalk*, 167.
3 Ibid., 168.
4 Ibid.

CHAPTER 21

1 "Gottschalk's being a former protégé of Ebbo [did] not endear him to the new archbishop of Reims." Genke, introduction to Genke and Gumerlock, *Gottschalk*, 40.
2 Ibid., 38.

CHAPTER 22

1 No. 326:3, in *The Psalter with Doctrinal Standards, Liturgy, Church Order, and added Chorale Section*, reprinted and revised edition of the 1912 United Presbyterian *Psalter* (Grand Rapids, MI: Eerdmans, 1927; rev. ed. 1995).
2 Although the parchments he had prepared did not survive, these were some of the main issues at stake, and this is the way these issues have been consistently answered throughout history. Gottschalk had shown himself to be remarkably consistent with what the later reformers of the sixteenth century argued concerning these issues. Francis Gumerlock observes that "the similarity between Gottschalk's statements on the bondage of the will, gracious ability, predestination, and redemption with those of the early Reformers, especially Calvin and his followers, is sometimes uncanny." Gumerlock, "Gottschalk of Orbais: A Medieval Predestinarian."
3 Hincmar of Reims, *Sentence against Gottschalk at the Synod of Quierzy*, trans. Francis X. Gumerlock, in Gumerlock in Genke and Gumerlock, *Gottschalk*, 169.
4 Schaff, *History of the Christian Church*, 4:528–29.

CHAPTER 23

1 See Genke and Gumerlock, *Gottschalk*, 71–96 and Hanko, "Gotteschalk's Doctrine of Double Predestination," 42–61.

CHAPTER 24

1 Hincmar, *Letter to Egilo*, trans. Victor Genke, in Genke and Gumerlock, *Gottschalk*, 43.

2   Hincmar, *Letter to the Monks and Simple Folk of his Diocese*, trans. Francis X.
    Gumerlock, in Genke and Gumerlock, *Gottschalk*, 169–72.
3   Genke, introduction to Genke and Gumerlock, *Gottschalk*, 46.

CHAPTER 25

1   Hincmar, *Letter to the Monks and Simple Folk of his Diocese*, trans. Francis X.
    Gumerlock, in Genke and Gumerlock, *Gottschalk*, 170.
2   Ibid.
3   Ibid., 171.
4   Gottschalk, *Tome to Gislemar*, trans. Victor Genke, in Genke and Gumerlock,
    Gottschalk, 69.
5   Canons of Dordt 5.15, in Schaff, *Creeds of Christendom*, 3:595.

CHAPTER 26

1   Hincmar, *Letter to Egilo*, trans. Victor Genke, in introduction to Genke and
    Gumerlock, *Gottschalk*, 43.
2   Ibid., 42.
3   Hanko, *Portraits of Faithful Saints*, 70–71.
4   "Becoming psychotic in the rather mild conditions, in which he was kept in
    Hautvillers, would be unlikely." Genke, introduction to Genke and Gumer-
    lock, *Gottschalk*, 43.
5   Tavard, *Trina Deitas*, 130n.
6   Schaff, *History of the Christian Church*, 4:529.
7   Adolph Harnack, *History of Dogma* (New York: Dover Publications, 1961),
    5:302n1.
8   Tavard, *Trina Deitas*, 126.
9   Neander, *General History*, 6:278.
10 Gottschalk, *Longer Confession*, trans. Francis Gumerlock, in Genke and
    Gumerlock, *Gottschalk*, 93.
11 Dales, *Intellectual Life of Western Europe*, 94.

CHAPTER 28

1   Gottschalk, *Longer Confession*, trans. Ronald Hanko, in Hanko, "Gotteschalk's
    Doctrine of Double Predestination," 47.

CHAPTER 30

2   Gottschalk, *Longer Confession*, trans. Ronald Hanko, in Hanko, "Gotte-
    schalk's Doctrine of Double Predestination," 49.
3   *Annals of St. Bertin*, trans. Victor Genke, in Genke and Gumerlock,
    Gottschalk, 53.

CHAPTER 31

1 Tavard, *Trina Deitas*, 127.

2 Gottschalk, *Longer Confession*, trans. Ronald Hanko, in Hanko, "Gotteschalk's Doctrine of Double Predestination," 53.

3 The exact year of Gottschalk's death is not known, but that it occurred on October 30 has been recorded.

4 Gottschalk, *Longer Confession*, trans. Ronald Hanko, in Hanko, "Gotteschalk's Doctrine of Double Predestination," 59.

APPENDIX 1

1 Conclusion to the Canons of Dordt, in Schaff, *Creeds of Christendom*, 3:596.

2 Gottschalk wrote a lengthy poem called "O my guardian" concerning his lament over his sins. Poem translated by Peter Godman in Godman, *Poetry of the Carolingian Renaissance*, 235.

3 Gottschalk, *Longer Confession*, trans. Ronald Hanko, in Hanko, "Gotteschalk's Doctrine of Double Predestination," 59.

4 A more literal translation can be found in Lawson, *Pillars of Grace*, 287, cited in Needham, *2,000 years of Christ's Power, Part Two*, 82.

5 Gottschalk, *Confessio Brevior* [Shorter Confession], in Hanko, "Gotteschalk's Doctrine of Double Predestination," 42–43.

BIBLIOGRAPHY

Armstrong, Dorsey. *The Medieval World* [transcript book]. Chantilly, VA: The Great Courses, 2009.

Baldwin, Marshall W. *The Mediaeval Church*. Ithaca, NY: Cornell University Press, 1953.

Bartlett, Kenneth R. *The Great Tours: Experiencing Medieval Europe* [recorded lectures]. Chantilly, VA: The Great Courses, 2013.

www.bistum-fulda.de: Art & Music

Calvin, John. *Calvin's Calvinism*. Jenison, MI: Reformed Free Publishing Association, 2009.

———. *Institutes of the Christian Religion*, vol. 2. Translated by Ford Lewis Battles. Philadelphia: The Westminster Press, 1960.

Catholic Encyclopedia: Hincmar, Archbishop of Reims, www.newadvent.org > Catholic Encyclopedia > Hincmar. May 21, 2015.

The Confessions and the Church Order of the Protestant Reformed Churches. Grandville, MI: Protestant Reformed Churches in America, 2005.

Daileader, Philip. *The Early Middle Ages* [recorded lectures]. Chantilly, VA: The Great Courses, 2004.

Dales, Richard C. *The Intellectual Life of Western Europe in the Middle Ages*. Washington, DC: University Press of America, 1980.

Danhof, Henry, and Herman Hoeksema. *Sin and Grace*. Translated by Cornelius Hanko. Grandville, MI: Reformed Free Publishing Association, 2003.

Duffield, Samuel Willoughby. *The Latin Hymn-Writers and their Hymns*. New York and London: Funk and Wagnalls, 1889.

Editors of Time-Life Books. *What Life Was Like in the Age of Chivalry: Medieval Europe AD 800-1500*. Richmond, VA: Time-Life Books, 1999.

Engelsma, David J. "A Defense of Calvinism as the Gospel." South Holland, IL: The Evangelism Committee [South Holland] Protestant Reformed Church, 1986.

Engelsma, David J., and Herman Hanko. *The Work of the Holy Spirit*. Muskegon, MI: British Reformed Fellowship, 2010.

Frassetto, Michael. *Encyclopedia of Barbarian Europe: Society in Transformation*. Santa Barbara, CA: ABC-CLIO, Inc., 2003.

Genke, Victor, and Francis X. Gumerlock, ed. and trans. *Gottschalk and a Medieval Predestination Controversy: Texts Translated from the Latin*. Milwaukee, WI: Marquette University Press, 2010.

———. *The Gottschalk Homepage*. http://gottschalk.inrebus.com/.

Godman, Peter. *Poetry of the Carolingian Renaissance*. London: Duckworth, 1985.

Gumerlock, Francis X. "Gottschalk of Orbais: A Medieval Predestinarian." http://www.kerux.com/kerux/doc/2203A4.asp.

———. "Predestination in the Century before Gottschalk. Part 1." *Evangelical Quarterly* 81:3 (July 2009).

———. "Predestination in the Century before Gottschalk. Part 2." *Evangelical Quarterly* 81:4 (October 2009).

Hanko, Herman. *Contending for the Faith: The Rise of Heresy and the Development of the Truth*. Jenison, MI: Reformed Free Publishing Association, 2010.

———. *Portraits of Faithful Saints*. Grandville, MI: Reformed Free Publishing Association, 1999.

Hanko, Ronald. *Doctrine According to Godliness*. Grandville, MI: Reformed Free Publishing Association, 2004.

———. "Gotteschalk's Doctrine of Double Predestination." *Protestant Reformed Theological Journal* 12:1 (November 1978).

Harnack, Adolph. *History of Dogma*. New York: Dover Publications, 1961.

Hoeksema, Herman. *Reformed Dogmatics,* vol. 2, 2nd ed. Grandville, MI: Reformed Free Publishing Association, 2005.

———. *The Triple Knowledge*, vol. 2. Grand Rapids, MI: Reformed Free Publishing Association, 1971.

Kenyon, Sherrilyn. *Everyday Life in the Middle Ages*. Cincinnati, OH: Writer's Digest Books, 1995.

Kurtz. *Church History*, vol. 1. London: Hodder and Stoughton, 1891.

Lawson, Steven J. *Pillars of Grace: A Long Line of Godly Men*. Lake Mary, FL: Reformation Trust Publishing, 2011.

McAleavy, Tony. *Life in a Medieval Abbey*. London: English Heritage, 1996.

McCracken, George E., ed. *Early Medieval Theology*. Library of Christian Classics, vol. 9. Louisville, KY: Westminster John Knox Press, 2006.

Monumenta Germaniae Historica, Poetae Latini Aevi Carolini, vol. 2. Ernst Duemmler, ed. 1884. 409–420.

Monumenta Germaniae Historica, Poetae Latini Aevi Carolini, vol. 3, *pars prior*. Ludwig Traube, ed. 1886. 724–738.

Monumenta Germaniae Historica, Nachträge Zu Den Poetae Aevi Carolini, vol. 6, 1. Karl Strecker, pub. 1951. 86–106.

Neander, Augustus. *General History of the Christian Religion and Church: From the German of Dr. Augustus Neander,* vol. 6. Translated by Joseph Torrey. Edinburgh: T. & T. Clark, 1850.

Ophoff, George M. "God's Sovereign Elective Grace." Lansing, IL: Peace Protestant Reformed Church, 1997.

Schaff, Philip, ed. *The Creeds of Christendom with a History and Critical Notes.* 6th ed. 3 vols. New York: Harper and Row, 1931; repr., Grand Rapids, MI: Baker Books, 2007.

———. *History of the Christian Church.* Vol. 4, *Mediaeval Christianity: From Gregory I to Gregory VII, AD 590–1073.*, Charles Scribner's Sons, 1910; repr. Grand Rapids, MI: William B. Eerdmans Publishing Company.

St. Benedict of Nursia. *St. Benedict's Rule for Monasteries.* Translated by Leonard J. Doyle. Collegeville, MN: The Liturgical Press, 1948.

Stucco, Guido. *God's Eternal Gift: A History of the Catholic Doctrine of Predestination from Augustine to the Renaissance.* USA: Xlibris Corporation, 2009.

Tavard, George H. *Trina Deitas: The Controversy between Hincmar and Gottschalk.* Milwaukee, WI: Marquette University Press, 1996.

Veldman, Herman. "The Doctrine of Sin, The Second Period—250–730 A.D., The Pelagian Controversy, Semi-Pelagianism." *Standard Bearer* 45, no. 1 (October 1, 1968).

———. "The Doctrine of Sin, The Second Period—250–730 A.D., The Pelagian Controversy, Semi-Pelagianism." *Standard Bearer* 45, no. 4 (November 15, 1968).

———. "The Doctrine of Sin, The Third Period—730–1517 A.D., Gottschalk." *Standard Bearer* 45, no. 5 (December 1, 1968).

PUBLIC DOMAIN
IMAGE CREDITS

CHAPTER 1
Charlemagne's throne at Aachen: photo by Bojin, Wikimedia Commons

CHAPTER 2
Coin depicting Charlemagne: photo by PHGCOM, Wikimedia Commons

CHAPTER 3
Fulda monastery and cathedral complex: photo by ThomasSD, Wikimedia Commons
Music of Gregorian chant: photo by Georges Jansoone, Wikimedia Commons

CHAPTER 4
St. Benedict's Rule: Wikimedia Commons

CHAPTER 5
Illuminated manuscript: Wikimedia Commons

CHAPTER 6
Reichenau: photo by Martin Steiger, Wikimedia Commons
Church of St. Michael: photo by Sven Teschke, Büdingen, Wikimedia Commons

CHAPTER 8
Crozier: Wikimedia Commons
Cloister: photo by Myrabella, Wikimedia Commons

CHAPTER 9
Artwork in a decorated copy of the Ebbo Gospels: Wikimedia Commons

CHAPTER 16
Cathedral in Mainz: photo by Moguntiner, Wikimedia Commons

CHAPTER 20
Cathedral in Reims: Wikimedia Commons

CHAPTER 23
Monastery in Hautvillers: photo by G. Garitan, Wikimedia Commons

Printed by Libri Plureos GmbH in Hamburg,
Germany